BRITAIN
AND THE
TWO WORLD WARS

Jocelyn Hunt
Head of History
Watford Girls' Grammar School
Hertfordshire

Sheila Watson
Head of History
Cheshunt School
Hertfordshire

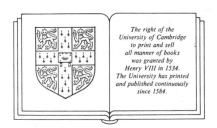

The right of the
University of Cambridge
to print and sell
all manner of books
was granted by
Henry VIII in 1534.
The University has printed
and published continuously
since 1584.

CAMBRIDGE UNIVERSITY PRESS

Cambridge   New York
Port Chester   Melbourne   Sydney

Published by the Press Syndicate of the University of Cambridge
The Pitt Building, Trumpington Street, Cambridge CB2 1RP
40 West 20th Street, New York, NY 10011, USA
10 Stamford Road, Oakleigh, Melbourne 3166, Australia

First published 1990

Printed in Great Britain at the University Press, Cambridge

British Library cataloguing-in-publication data
Hunt, Jocelyn
Britain and the two world wars – (Cambridge Topics in History.)
1. Great Britain. Social conditions. Effects of World War 1.
2. Great Britain. Social conditions. Social conditions in Great Britain. Effects of World War 2.
I. Title II. Watson, Sheila
941.083

Library of Congress cataloging-in-publication data
Hunt, Jocelyn,
  Britain and the two world wars/Jocelyn Hunt, Sheila Watson.
    p. cm.
    Bibliography: p.
    Includes index.
    ISBN 0-521-36953-3
    1. World War, 1914–1918 — Great Britain. 2. Great Britain–History — George V, 1910–1936. 3. World War, 1939–1945 — Great Britain. 4. Great Britain–History — George VI, 1936–1952.
I. Watson, Sheila. II. Title.
DA577.H86 1990
940.3'41–dc20   89-36123 CIP

ISBN 0 521 36953 3

US

Contents

Acknowledgements

The authors and publisher would like to thank the following for permission to reproduce extracts and illustrations:

Extracts   1.4, 1.15, 1.16, 1.17, 5.1 *Hansard* © of Parliament; 1.5 Lord Beaverbrook, *Politicians and the War 1914–1916*, 1928, Methuen, London; 1.6, 1.7, 1.9, 1.10 D. Boulton, *Objection Overruled*; 1.12, 1.13, 1.18 E. David (ed.), *Inside Asquith's Cabinet*, 1977, John Murray (Publishers) Ltd.; 1.14 C. Hazlehurst, *Politicians at War, July 1914– May 1915*, 1971; 1.20, 2.4, 4.5 Frances Stevenson, *Lloyd George: A Diary*, edited by A. J. P. Taylor, 1917, Hutchinson; 1.22, 1.23, 1.24 R. J. Scally, *Origins of the Lloyd George Coalition*, 1975, Princeton University Press; 2.1, 2.7 (derived from), 2.8 A. S. Milward, *Economic Effects of the Two World Wars on Britain*, 1984, 6.12 Corelli Barnett, *The Audit of War*, 1986, Macmillan, London and Basingstoke; 2.6, 2.7 (derived from) R. W. Breach and R. M. Hartwell, *British Economy and Society, 1870–1970*, 1972, 2.9 W. Beveridge, *Some Experiences of Economic Control in Wartime*, 1940, Oxford University Press; 3.4, 3.5, 3.9, 3.10, 7.10, 7.11, 7.12, 8.1, 8.4, 8.6, 8.9, 8.10, 8.11 Public Record Office; 3.6(a) *The Manchester Guardian*; 3.6(c) *The Daily Mail*; 3.8, 3.15 *The Times*; 4.4 N. Reeves, *Official British Film Propaganda during World War I*, 1986, 6.9 S. Pollard, *The Wasting of the British Economy*, 1984, Croom Helm; D. Mason, *Churchill 1914–1918*, 1973, © Ballantine Books; 5.6 reprinted from D. Day, *Menzies and Churchill*, 1986, by kind permission of the publishers, Angus & Robertson; 5.7, 5.8(a), 5.8(b) B. Pimlott (ed.), *The Second World War Diaries of Hugh Dalton 1940–1945*, 1986, The British Library of Political and Economic Science, Jonathan Cape Ltd; 5.10 Sir John Colville, *The Fringes of Power*, 1985, Hodder and Stoughton and W. W. Norton & Company Inc.; 5.11 Winston Churchill, *The Second World War*, vol. 3, *The Grand Alliance*, 1950, Cassell plc; 6.1 A. Sked, *Britain's Decline*, 1987, Basil Blackwell Ltd; 6.3–6.7 adapted from W. K. Hancock and M. M. Gouring, *The British War Economy*, 1949, 6.8 M. M. Postan, *British War Production*, 1952, Controller of Her Majesty's Stationery Office; 7.1 *Cambridge Daily News*, 1 September 1939 – now the *Cambridge Evening News*; 7.5 taken from *No Time to Wave Goodbye* by Ben Wicks, published by Bloomsbury Publishing Limited; 7.7, 7.17(a), 7.17(b), 7.17(c) Mass-Observation, *The Journey Home*, 1944, 8.7 Mass-Observation file report no. 224, © The Tom Harrisson Mass-Observation Archive. Reproduced by permission of Curtis Brown Ltd; 7.9 from *The Ordeal of Total War, 1939–1945* by Gordon Wright. Copyright © 1968 by Gordon Wright. Reprinted by permission of Harper & Row, Publishers Inc.; 7.16 *Woman*, 8 December 1945, Solo Syndication & Literary Agency Ltd; 8.2 J. C. W. Reith, *Into the Wind*, 1949, Peters, Fraser & Dunlop; Alfred Duff Cooper, *Old Men Forget*, 1954, Grafton Books; 8.8 © *The Daily Telegraph* plc.

Illustrations   2.2, 3.1(a), 3.1(b), 3.2(a), 3.2(b), 4.1, 5.5, 7.13, 8.5 The Trustees of the Imperial War Museum, London; 5.9 David Low, Associated Newspapers plc.; 7.2 *Cambridge Daily News*, 1 September 1939 – now the *Cambridge Evening News*; 7.14 *Punch*.

Cover illustration   Details from cartoons in *Punch, or the London Charivari*, showing the key wartime Prime Ministers, Lloyd George, *Punch*, 28 July 1915 (before he became Prime Minister), and Churchill, *Punch*, 1 October 1941.

Every effort has been made to reach copyright holders; the publishers would be pleased to hear from anyone whose rights they have unwittingly infringed.

Introduction

The purpose of this book is to enable students to see for themselves some examples of the vast range of sources available to historians of the First and Second World Wars, and the impact these wars had on Britain. Although this book does not set out to give an account of the events of the wars, nor indeed every aspect of the home front, this Introduction does offer a brief account of the main issues and developments at home, in order to provide the reader with a context in which to study the individual themes. Comparison of the two wars is neither the purpose nor an over-riding theme, because students may be studying one without the other; however, the four pairs of central chapters will enable the reader to detect some parallels and differences, and the Introduction provides an overall comparison. It also draws attention to the Marwick Thesis.

The Marwick Thesis

This Thesis[1] has been chosen as an example of the way in which historians have attempted to rationalise the long- and short-term consequences of the wars on Britain. Marwick is one of the few historians who attempts to analyse all aspects of the British wartime experience using models. Readers will probably have met some of the other, more traditional approaches to tackling the history of the two world wars, a few of which are summarised below:

(i) The anecdotal approach (Oral History). This involves the comprehensive presentation of primary accounts with some analysis of trends. A good recent example is Ben Wicks' *No Time to Wave Goodbye*, 1988, an account of evacuation in the Second World War.

(ii) The statistical approach. This reflects an attempt to understand war by measuring all the changes taking place.

(iii) The 'broad sweep' approach. In this case, the wars are usually only slotted into wider surveys of twentieth-century history and mentioned as confirming or delaying longer-term developments.

(iv) The 'doom and despondency' approach. Here, the history of Britain in the twentieth century is seen as one of inevitable decline on all fronts with the two wars merely accelerating the trend.

(v) The patriotic approach. This is exemplified by Churchill's own histories where the tendency is to use the wars as demonstrations of British courage, inventiveness, tenacity and ability to improvise.

The reader should be aware of the different types of historiographic *genres* which have influenced historians. Marwick has categorised them into four main types: 'tory'; 'liberal'; 'economic'; and 'sociological'.[1] The tory approach is among the oldest, but still has its adherents. It sees war in terms of strategies and difficulties and tends to see the effect of war on society solely as a pressure forcing central administration to adopt more responsibility towards directing civilian lives. It regards war as productive in that it stimulates patriotism, inventiveness and social cohesion. Liberal historians take the opposite view. War is seen as essentially undesirable, suppressing, as they see it, civil liberties, and encouraging propaganda, and a breakdown of social and political stability amounting to the collapse of civilisation. The economists concentrate upon the way in which war changes the economic basis of society, or exposes the weaknesses of pre-war society and economic planning. Sociologists concentrate upon the effect that war has on class, and the economic and social status of groups within society.

Marwick also presents an interesting method of assessing the impact of war by breaking it down into four aspects: destructive/disruptive; test; participation; and psychological. The first (destructive and disruptive) appears, perhaps, the easiest to come to terms with. Everyone agrees that war destroys something – factories, houses, people – and causes massive expenditure. Marwick points out, however, that the results of such devastation may not always be negative. Catastrophies sometimes prompt the human species to rethink its habits and to rebuild and reconstruct in new or better ways. In both wars we can, perhaps, see this kind of effect in an area such as the growth of the Welfare State.

The second aspect, test, concentrates on analysing how well the political, social and economic structure of society survives the test of war. Both wars appear to have had a conservative effect upon Britain and her institutions. The structure of politics appeared malleable enough to adjust surprisingly well to the exigencies of war. Parliament adapted to the new situation, producing (albeit with some strain between and within the political parties) united governments which only extended their control over peoples' lives where there was general consent and approval. Society, too, emerged little changed from the wars. Long-term trends, such as increased geographical and social mobility, may have been accelerated, but the cultural, economic and educational divisions between groups in society were probably less diminished by the wartime experience than by the extension of the mass media, and by the rising standard of living of the lower and middle sections of society, which have characterised most decades of the twentieth century.

The effect of the 'test' aspect on British society is linked to the third, 'participation', aspect. Marwick has argued that the two world wars involved all groups in society and this widened social aspirations; at the same time there were increased opportunities for greater economic rewards. Both wars led to social reforms and a higher standard of living for the lower classes in society, relative to those above them on the social scale.

The fourth aspect is the psychological experience of war – the way that conflict changes people's perceptions of themselves, society, the arts and religion. Again, the two wars appear to have produced little that was revolutionary. In art, literature, music, drama, philosophy and theology, Robbins[2] has argued that it is difficult to see the first war inspiring developments and ideas for which there were no pre-1914 precedents. Nor did the second war jolt intellectual attitudes into new lines. If anything, it saw a retreat into earlier conformity, with classical music, literature and art all enjoying a revival. People wanted to be reassured in wartime that something of the pre-war world remained. It was in science and technology that developments were greater, but these owed less to new intellectual attitudes than to the demands of war, and were themselves but extensions, albeit accelerated ones, of a movement which has marked the twentieth century as a whole.

A comparison between the two world wars

For civilians and soldiers alike, the two world wars proved to be radically different experiences.

The key to the differences lies in the nature of the two wars.[3] For the soldier, the First World War was a war of attrition. It became a slogging contest between well-matched armies, with wanton loss of life, interspersed with long periods of relative inactivity in demoralising trenches. When the fighting began it was arduous, prolonged and horrific. The first major British offensive of the war, Neuve Chapelle, March 1915, lasted three days. 1,200 yards (1,000 m) of land were gained at a cost of 13,000 British and 12,000 German casualties. Shocking though these figures are, they were relatively light compared with later equally fruitless but longer-lasting operations.

For the people at home fortunate enough not to have menfolk in the armed forces the war was, at first, little more than an inconvenience. The British public, spared the horrors of invasion and, with the exception of a few Zeppelin raids (1915–18), the destruction of bombing, adapted themselves slowly to the changing demands of war. The most obvious impact that the war made was on the numbers of men of military age out of the country. Over one million had volunteered by the end of 1914, and this had risen to 2.5 million by the following year. In 1918 there were 3.8 million members of the armed forces training or fighting abroad. In the four years of the war three quarters of a million British men died in action or later as a result of wounds. Approximately one and a half million men suffered permanent injury.[4] (This was out of a total male population of about 22 million.) Men in essential war work such as manufacturing and mining were allowed to enlist; their places were taken partly by allowing the dilution of labour (use of unskilled labour) and partly by women. By July 1918, 4.9 million women were in paid employment, compared with 3.3 million in 1914. As these figures show, the war was important not so much for the employment of women *per se*, but for the type of job it opened up for them. Thousands left domestic service for the greater freedom and increased financial rewards of factory or similar war work.

The government proved reluctant to increase its powers over the British war effort, but mounting criticism of its incompetence and the inexorable demands of the military, who gauged the chances of success in terms of quantities of ammunition and bombs expended as well as numbers of men in the field, forced the introduction of controls. The Munitions of War Act, July 1915, gave the government greater powers than ever before to control labour by forbidding strikes and lockouts and ending restrictive practices in certain factories. Workers' rights to leave jobs were curtailed. Slowly government powers were extended over almost all essential wartime industries. Five new departments were created, to supervise shipping, food, food production, labour and national service. They co-operated with major manufacturers and, by the end of the war, state control extended to areas such as transport, agriculture, mining and certain industries (such as chemicals) in a manner inconceivable four years before.

For most, the end justified the means. The British economy, mobilised for war, produced, after the munitions crisis of 1915, all the supplies the military needed. For example, at Passchendaele in 1917, 4 million shells were fired at the Germans in 10 days. On one day alone, in September 1918, the British lines fired 943,000 shells, costing £3.87 million. There was a heavy price to pay for this. The war cost Britain £11,325 million; about a third of this was paid for by a greatly increased income tax and an excess profits duty, but the rest was borrowed.

Britain's legacy from the war was an increased National Debt and a worsening balance of payments. However, thanks to invisible earnings, Britain's current account was, on average, £50 million per annum in the black during the war. Although this was a great reduction from the £181 million of 1913, it was enough to protect the sterling exchange rate.[5] Unfortunately, the government failed to realise that Britain's economy had been weakened in other ways by the war: markets had been lost; too much investment had been placed into the old staple industries such as shipbuilding and, despite the stimulation of war, not enough into the newer ones such as chemicals and electricity. Consequently, when Britain returned to the Gold Standard in 1925, the pound was over-valued and trade competition became even more difficult.

Yet we should not over-estimate the damage done to Britain's economy by the war. Although the post-war boom ended in a slump in 1921, it has been claimed[6] that, with the exception of the years between 1929 and 1932, the British economy grew more strongly than before 1914 and more strongly, moreover, than that of many of her industrial competitors.

Only towards the end of the war did the British public suffer serious economic inconvenience, with shortages and food rationing of a more than temporary duration. 'Business as usual' was the proud boast of many shops and firms in the last quarter of 1914. By 1918, however, all civilians were affected by rationing, price rises and shortages. The government proved reluctant to intervene against market forces. Not until November 1916 was the appointment of a Food Controller announced, and even then most measures at first depended upon a voluntary reduction in the consumption of luxuries. Queues and local shortages forced the government to act. By May 1918, adults were rationed to three quarters of a pound of meat per week. Other items rationed included sugar, tea, butter and margarine. The prices of bread and potatoes were controlled. Milk rationing was introduced after the armistice, and meat, butter and sugar did not come off the ration until October 1919, or later.

Civilians were affected as much by inflation as rationing. By 1918, the retail price index had risen from a base of 100 in July 1914 to 203. Yet wages rose as fast, if not faster, in many households, boosted by increased opportunities for overtime. Consumer spending statistics suggest only a marginal reduction in living standards. Expenditure fell by 20% between 1913 and 1918; one quarter of this decline was on food, one quarter on clothing and one third on alcohol. The nutritional standard of the diet was almost the same as before the war.[7] The effects of these economic trends were not uniform; there were, no doubt, many households whose real standard of living was eroded by the wartime experience but for many, especially those in the working classes, the evidence suggests some improvement.

In this respect, the Second World War repeated the pattern of the First. By 1943, national income was 64% higher than it had been in 1939.[8] This was due to increased employment prospects and subsidies which curbed inflation. After a slow start, which resembled the lack of urgency seen in 1914, the government adopted sweeping powers to mobilise the population. Bevin, Minister of Labour, persuaded the unions to accept dilution of labour, in an arrangement similar to Lloyd George's Treasury Agreement of 1915. In March 1941, skilled workers had to register and the government was empowered to direct them to undertake essential war work. Women were also registered and, by the end of the war, many of them had been directed to war work. By 1943, the employed population had increased by 2.9 million, absorbing the 700,000 who had still been out of work in mid-1940. Bevin, a trade unionist with the welfare of workers as a priority, ensured that standards of wages, conditions and benefits were maintained, and, in many cases, improved. In order to avoid inflation of the First World War kind, Kingsley Wood's budget of April 1941 restricted price increases on essential goods, to keep increases in the cost of living index to not more than 25-30% of the pre-war level.

There was far less on which to spend increased income in the Second World War. Learning from previous experience, rationing of foods began early in the war; among the first items were sugar and bacon. Meat, tea, fats and margarine were all rationed in 1940, cheese from mid-1941, while many foods became scarce or unobtainable. Clothes were rationed in June 1941, and control of raw materials restricted very severely the number of consumer goods available.

Yet these statistics only hint at the different civilian experience of the two wars. Besides increased severity of rationing and more stringent control of labour, the British public on the home front suffered disruption of their lives, physical danger and the day-to-day experience of war in a way unknown twenty years before. Few people at home between 1914 and 1918 could begin to comprehend the horrors of trench warfare for, despite the availability of some realistic cinema footage, patriotic newspaper reporting, assisted by censorship, glossed over the nightmare experience.

A generation later, censorship again prevented the publication of photographs of large numbers of mutilated bodies after the Blitz; patriotic newspapers reported little of the gross reality of smashed houses and distraught victims, concentrating instead on the rescue services and the determination of the population to go on fighting. However, no exhortatory propaganda, no number of published photographs or newsreel clips of smiling Blitz survivors and their rescuers, no uninformative BBC announcements of raids could lessen for a moment the trauma, anguish and terror suffered by many civilians. Nor could cheerful posters and bracing radio talks soften the misery of evacuation, the monotony of rations, the gloom of the blackout and the exhaustion of long hours of war work. In almost every field of human experience, the Second War dealt a harsher blow to the people of Britain than the First.

It is difficult to say whether detestation of Hitler and Fascism was more uniform in 1939 than loathing of the Kaiser and the bullying tactics of German militarism had been in 1914; there is no doubt, however, that the threat of invasion in 1940 united people in the face of common danger. Partly also, the government, learning from the mistakes of the Great War, established, much earlier than in the previous conflict, departments to control and supervise all aspects of food, work, evacuation and transport. The public was also better informed, as newsreels presented them with far more realistic images of war than the newspapers of 1914–18 had done. Independent of direct government control, the BBC retained its image of impartial integrity while, at the same time, since it depended heavily on government departments for news and information and submitted itself to voluntary censorship, it rarely deviated from the muted patriotic tone which the British public grew to appreciate and from which they took courage. Churchill, reluctant though he was to use the new media, nevertheless benefited from its adulatory portrayal of his leadership; and his voice, mannerisms and strength of purpose, promoted by the media, made him more popular even than Lloyd George. The workers, protected by Bevin's concern for welfare and wages, and seeing Labour ministers actively concerned with home affairs in a coalition government, buried their 1920s' dislike of Churchill and trusted that no-one was benefiting from the war in the way that certain industrialists had appeared to do in the previous one.

In another important area, the experience of the Second War did not mirror that of the First. 270,000 military casualties were themselves a depressing enough figure but, when compared to the 745,000 of 1914–18, they seemed miraculously light. Far fewer families mourned in the second war, though many more had their own lives disrupted.

In the sphere of finance, it appeared at first as though the lessons of the Great War had not been learned.[9] Chamberlain's government hoped that increased taxation and an export drive would pay for the war. The military crisis of May and June 1940 and the advent of the Churchill ministry marked a new, grim realism in British economic strategy. Government expenditure rose from £1,408 million in 1939–40, to £6,180 million in 1944–5 and the percentage spent on defence during this period rose from 45 per cent to 83 per cent. 'Victory at all costs' was paid for by the sales of foreign investments, borrowing, under-investment in non-essential industries, and by the population through increased taxation, compulsory savings schemes, rationing, increased working hours and fewer luxuries. The war cost £28,000 million, 2.5 times the cost of the Great War. By 1945, Britain was £3,500 million in debt, compared with £496 million in 1939. Her overseas markets were reduced, her industries under-funded and her reserves spent. She survived the immediate post-war era on loans from the USA and Canada, by austerity, and by devaluing sterling in 1949 from $4.03 to $2.08. Yet there were, as in the first war, considerable technological gains. Just as the earlier conflict stimulated developments in transport and medicine, so the second encouraged the growth of chemicals, electronics, aircraft and road transport, and marked the emergence of British farming from the inter-war depression into a new era of efficiency, productivity and prosperity.

Both wars witnessed an increased demand for social reforms. The memory of a betrayed generation, of the failure to build 'homes fit for heroes', of ex-servicemen begging for jobs, all reinforced the determination felt in the early 1940s that equality of sacrifice in wartime should be matched by a reduction in the inequalities of peacetime. This resolve was given expression in the post-war Labour government's legislation which nationalised key industries, set up the National Health Service and widened the scope of welfare provision. Both wars, however, merely accelerated a trend which had its origins in the Liberal reforms of the period 1905–14, a trend which had continued, though in weakened form, in the legislation of the inter-war years which extended the Pension Scheme (1925) and set up the Public Assistance Board (1934–5). In the same way, the massive increase in state control over all areas of the economy and society which both wars, though particularly the Second one, witnessed, may be seen as speeding up a tendency displayed by all twentieth-century governments until 1979. The Second World War, learning from the First, is a clear example of what Middlemass has termed the development of the 'corporate bias', 'the tendency of industrial, trade union and financial institutions to make reciprocal arrangements with each other and the government' to avoid overt conflict.[10]

In recent years, an improvement in Britain's economic performance and pressures on the social reforms of the 1940s, have led to reassessments of the consequences of the 1939–45 conflict for Britain. These make a direct comparison of the long-term effects of those wars more tentative than those written even five years ago. While both wars, as we have seen, saw a widening of government controls over the economy and society, after 1918 most of these were rapidly dismantled in the scramble to return to pre-war conditions. In contrast, the retention and extension of such powers after 1945, to provide the means by which the economy could be centrally managed and society supplied with comprehensive and universal welfare services, was seen as the permanent legacy of the experience of 1939–45. However, even if these changes, including the nationalisation of major industries, the commitment to full employment and the Welfare State, have proved less durable than historians, until recently, predicted, nevertheless it remains true that one of the most significant differences between the two wars was the way that, following the disappointed expectations of the First War, the Second resulted in a long-term acceptance that government controls could and should be used to provide a framework for social planning, in a form undreamed of in 1939.

Propaganda was another area in which the second war differed significantly from the first. The excesses of atrocity propaganda in the First World War led to a rather shame-faced attitude in the Second and, although both wars started from the same assumption that morale was something which could be manipulated, it was only in the Second World War that attempts were made to measure it. In both, support for the war remained high, and in neither war did government-inspired morale-raising efforts play a significant part in civilian determination to go on fighting.

At first glance, the impact of the two wars on British politics appears similar, both in incidental detail and in wider implications. Both wars brought about a weakening of the leading party on the outbreak of war; in both wars, charismatic leaders emerged to pilot the nation through apparently insurmountable difficulties to triumphant victory. In this, the Second World War had a more old-fashioned look than the First. Churchill was unquestionably a member of the ruling classes, whereas Lloyd George was a 'jumped up' Welsh Radical. It has been suggested that Blenheim and Harrow gave the former confidence which the latter was often seen to lack.[11] Both leaders were single minded about the war, though advances in transport and communications enabled Churchill to become much more directly involved in the fighting than Lloyd George. Both were willing to argue with their military specialists, although Lloyd George is reputed to have over-ruled them more often than Churchill. They were both in similar political positions, and Churchill set up a War Cabinet on the Lloyd George model. It seems probable that Lloyd George listened to his colleagues as equals more than Churchill did; on the other hand, Lloyd George was more prepared to go against their advice. It was the First World War and not the Second which broke the mould of British politics.[12] The Liberals never recovered from their split of 1916 and, with the disappearance of the Irish Nationalists as a force at Westminster, the House of Commons became, in effect, the preserve of the Conservative Party until 1945.

If the First World War saw the death of the Liberal Party, the Second marked the coming of age of Labour as a credible party of government. The Second World War gave Labour not only ministerial experience, but also a mandate from the people for large-scale socialism. At the same time, the Conservative Party emerged united in a way which had seemed impossible in May 1940, thanks to the magnanimity of Churchill and to Chamberlain's honourable behaviour. As Lloyd George himself remarked of Churchill, 'He will not smash the Tory Party to save the country as I smashed the Liberal Party'.[13] Churchill's reward was a party base upon whose shoulders he could return to power at the age of 76 in 1951. Lloyd George, on the other hand, allowed the Liberal Party to split so completely that it never recovered; and at the end of the wartime coalition, the lack of a party base effectively ended his career in politics.

Yet finally, despite all the evidence of change, one must conclude that the two world wars tended to preserve and strengthen traditional social, political and economic institutions in Britain. By winning wars, the British system of government demonstrated its competence. The faces in the Commons may have changed in 1919 and 1945, but the structure of politics, the role of the Prime Minister in Cabinet, political differences rationalised into a party system, had not. Both wars provided all sections of society with a shared goal and, on the home front as on battlefields worldwide, a common sense of sacrifice. At the same time, by lessening, however slightly, the economic differences between the classes (a trend more visible in the Second War than in the First) and by offering greater employment prospects, both wars helped to ensure that Britain's traditional social structure survived intact, unassailed by the threat of class war or revolution. If change was caused by war it was, perhaps, by the way in which the feeling of common purpose and shared experience sanctioned the reforms of the Labour governments after 1945. Now, as the memory of war fades, those reforms are no longer seen as permanent. What once seemed fundamental and inevitable changes in the way society regarded itself, and the government its responsibilites, are now seeming more and more to have been temporary, though long-lasting, post-war aberrations.

In selecting the extracts that follow, we have attempted to provide readers with a range of material which will assist them in developing the skills of historians. For this reason, we have chosen clusters of thematically linked sources. This, we hope, will enable students to appreciate the processes by which historians arrive at generalisations and draw conclusions. Some of these sources, particularly those based on numerical and statistical material, may prove to be especially suitable for group discussion.

References

1 See A. Marwick, *War and Social Change in the Twentieth Century*, Macmillan, 1974

2 K. Robbins, *The First World War*, OUP, 1984, p. 164

3 For much of the statistical information, we are indebted to P. Dewey, 'The New Warfare and Economic Mobilisation' in J. Turner (ed.), *Britain and the First World War*, Unwin Hyman, 1988, paperback edn; J. Stevenson, *British Society 1914–45*, Penguin, 1984; and H. Pelling, *Britain and the Second World War*, Fontana, 1979

4 A. J. P. Taylor, *English History 1914–45*, Pelican, 1970, p.165

5 P. Dewey, 'The New Warfare and Economic Mobilisation' in J. Turner (ed.), *Britain and the First World War*, Unwin Hyman, 1988, p.83

6 J. Turner (ed.), Introduction, in *Britain and the First World War*, Unwin Hyman, 1988, p.13

7 P. Dewey, 'Food Consumption in the United Kingdom 1914–18' in R. Wall and J. M. Winter (eds.), *The Upheaval of War*, CUP, 1987

8 A. S. Milward, *War, Economy and Society 1939–45*, Allen Lane, 1977, Pelican edn, 1987, p.89

9 Most of the information and arguments arising from it are from J. Stevenson, *British Society 1914–45*, Penguin, 1984

10 K. Middlemass, *Power, Competition and the State*, Macmillan, 1986, p.1

11 J. Ehrman, *Transactions of the Royal Historical Society*, 1961, pp.101ff

12 J. Turner, 'British Politics and the Great War', in J. Turner (ed.), *Britain and the First World War*, Unwin Hyman, 1988, p.117

13 T. Jones, *Lloyd George*, OUP, 1951, pp.464–5

1 Government and politics in the First World War

The First World War is credited with – or blamed for – bringing about some of the greatest political changes Britain has ever seen. This chapter attempts to introduce some of the enormous range of sources from which have emerged the various generalisations with which the student is familiar. It considers briefly the way each of the three key political parties fared in the war.

The Conservative Party: marking time?

The Conservative Party was in Opposition as the war began. The two General Elections of 1910 had reversed the 'landslide' Liberal victory of 1906, and the Liberals were only in power by courtesy of the Irish Nationalists and the infant Labour Party. It might have been expected that the Conservatives would aim to take over conduct of the war, or at least to play some part in it, and indeed, many individuals did express hopes of this kind. Lord Curzon, for example, wrote in 1914: 'When the war broke out, I offered myself to Asquith for non-political work in any capacity. But none has been offered to me.'[1]

Robert Blake[2] comments on the background to this feeling:

> On almost every issue that came up, Conservative tradition and ideology was better suited than Liberal to meet the needs of the hour ... All the necessities of a prolonged war tended to create doubts and divisions in the Liberals. After all, they were the party of liberty, and liberty is the first casualty of war. They were the party of moral conscience – and that is another casualty of war ... It was the Conservatives who before the war had been anti-German, who had pressed for conscription, for greater armaments, for a tougher foreign policy.

When eventually they did play a part in coalition, first under Asquith and then Lloyd George, the Conservatives performed their subordinate parts readily. Blake comments:[2]

The convulsion of December 1916 and the emergence of Lloyd George ... was another step forward politically for the Conservatives, who dominated the new coalition ... the leading Conservatives, however suspicious, were prepared to serve under a Prime Minister who, in spite of his defects, was an indubitable fighter and who cared   5 nothing for the traditional Liberal shibboleths if they interfered with the remorseless prosecution of the war.

But, given that they 'dominated' the Coalition, it seems hard to explain why they did not take the lead earlier, unless the cynical view is accepted, which suggests that they recognised that the Liberal Party would tear itself apart far more effectively in Government than in Opposition, and thus they would have a clear field in the post-war years. Extracts 1.1 to 1.5 enable the reader to find other reasons for the Conservatives 'marking time', rather than seizing the initiative.

Asquith recollected:

1.1   15 July 1914

I had a short talk with B[Bonar] Law. I pointed out that a failure to settle [in fact, the question of Ireland] would mean a general election with a very difficult situation at the end of it for whoever is victorious.

H. H. Asquith, *Memories and Reflections*, Vol 2, 1928

1.2

Even before the reconstruction of the government by the formation of the first Coalition in May 1915 it had been found expedient from time to time to enter into confidential communication with the leaders of the Opposition on matters upon which in normal conditions the Cabinet would have acted entirely upon its own   5 judgement.

H. H. Asquith, *Memories and Reflections*, Vol 2, 1928

1.3   14 Sept 1914

This afternoon has been quite dramatic. I made a quiet, rather humdrum speech [on the suspension of the Home Rule Act], pitched purposely in a low key, which was well listened to by the Tories as a

whole. Then Bonar Law followed with his usual indictment of us,
and me in particular, for lying and breaking faith, treachery etc.   5
several of the Irish and of our Radicals went and sat on the opposition benches.

H. H. Asquith, *Memories and Reflections***, Vol 2, 1928**

1.4   Lord Curzon in the House of Lords, 6 January 1915

We, as an Opposition, are in a rather peculiar position in this war.
We have no share either in official responsibility or in executive
authority in connection with the war. Many of us – myself, for in-
stance, know little more about it than the man in the street ... But
the fact that we know so little and have no authority does not deter   5
us for one moment from giving His Majesty's ministers, as we have
done and shall continue to do, the most unstinted support. And,
whilst speaking of that support, I should like to say here, what I
know to be true, that on many occasions, we on this side, both in
Parliament and in public, have refrained from making speeches and   10
from asking questions, where speech was tempting and where criticism would have been easy.

*Hansard, House of Lords***, Vol 18, col 238**

1.5   Lord Beaverbrook's view

Bonar Law's position was completely self consistent ... he had no
abstract objection to Coalition. On the contrary he thought it was the
form of government to which a long and severe war must inevitably
bring the nation. But he considered this to be the last step to take
and not the first. So long as a Liberal Government had credit for   5
success and good management and a patriotic Opposition was content
not to oppose, all was well.

When one considers how, in the course of the four years of war,
the capacity and credit of Ministry after Ministry was exhausted, it is
clear that Bonar Law showed a penetration into the future which   10
exceeded that of most of his contemporaries in the fateful summer of
1914 ...

There were many members of his party who were deeply disappointed at not being able to serve in a war government. They had to

content themselves as it was with very minor positions of service,   15
while they considered that their talents gave them the right to higher
places which they could fill to better advantage to the country than
the Liberal occupant. But the movement was checked at the very
outset by the clear and unalterable view expressed by Bonar Law that
he was opposed to Coalition. As long as the leader was of this   20
opinion, colleagues or followers could really effect nothing in the
contrary direction.

Lord Beaverbrook, *Politicians and the War 1914–16*, 1928

Questions

1   What is the implication of document 1.1? Why would this be a more
     significant threat in time of war?
2   How far does 1.2 indicate that informal steps towards Coalition were
     being taken in the early months of the war? Compare the views
     expressed in 1.2 with those stated in 1.4.
3   The story of Ireland is critical in any understanding of the period.
     Make sure that you know how the Unionists and the Liberals felt
     about the Irish question before commenting on 1.3. Why might the
     Conservatives prefer not to be in government during the settlement
     of the Irish question for the duration of the war?
4   Explain the two Conservative views expressed in 1.4 and 1.5.
5   In considering all these extracts [1.1–1.5], which clues to the inaction
     of the Conservatives do you find most convincing, and why?
6   Evaluate sources 1.1–1.5 in terms of date, author and reliability.
     Which do you feel is reporting at a distance? What are the credentials
     of each of the people quoted here which give them a value for the
     student of the period?

Whatever the reasons for the inaction of the Conservative Party in the
early months of the war, they emerged as ultimate beneficiaries of the
split in the Liberal Party, as did the Labour Party.

The rest of this chapter considers two further generalisations about
politics in the First World War, namely that the war brought about the
emergence to real significance of the Labour Party; and that it caused the
death of the Liberal Party, which never formed another government after
1915. The 'death of the Liberal Party' also forms the backdrop for one of
the great personal confrontations of political history – Asquith falling to
the cunning of Lloyd George.

The Labour Party: changing fortunes

The development of the Labour Party during the Great War is expounded very clearly by Paul Adelman.[3] There are a number of key issues. Did the war bring about the arrival of British Socialism, or was the war merely an accelerator of existing trends? How did the Labour Party survive the war at all, considering it entered it with very divided attitudes to the conflict? Indeed, the differences of opinion in August 1914 might have been expected to destroy the Party completely.

Consider the following views:

1.6   Labour Party Executive Resolution, 5 August 1914

[The government's] duty is now to secure peace at the earliest possible moment on such conditions as will produce the best opportunities for the re-establishment of amicable feelings between the workers of Europe.

Quoted in David Boulton, *Objection Overruled*, 1967

1.7   Statement by the National Administrative Council of ILP (Independent Labour Party), in *Labour Leader*, 13 August 1914

We are told that international socialism is dead, that all our hopes and ideals are wrecked by the fire and pestilence of European War. It is not true. Out of the darkness and the depth, we hail our working class comrades of every land. Across the roar of guns we send sympathy and greetings to the German Socialists. They have   5
laboured unceasingly to promote good relations with Britain as we with Germany. They are no enemies of ours, but faithful friends.

Quoted in David Boulton, *Objection Overruled*, 1967

1.8   An economist writes:

At any moment the government and the capitalists whom they represent will be able to abrogate all the laws on the plea of 'National Emergency'. If Labour continues throughout the war to allow gains won by industrial warfare in time of international peace to be filched from it, it is laying up a store of misery and hardship in the future.   5
All the old battles will have to be fought over again, and instead of being further on the road to emancipation, Labour will have lost ground.

G. D. H. Cole in the *Daily Herald*, 20 August 1914

1.9   Resolution of the Parliamentary Committee of Trade Unions, GFTU Management Committee and National Executive of Labour Party, 24 August 1914

[Resolution] that an immediate effort be made to terminate all existing trade disputes, whether strikes or lock outs and whenever new points of difficulty arise during the war period, a serious attempt should be made by all concerned to reach an amicable settlement before resorting to a strike or lock-out.   5

Quoted in David Boulton, *Objection Overruled,* **1967**

1.10   Resolution of the National Executive of the Labour Party (ILP dissenting), 29 August 1914

[Resolution] that in view of the serious situation created by the European war, the Executive Committee of the Labour Party agrees with the policy of the Parliamentary Party in joining in the Campaign to strengthen the British Army and agrees to place the Central Office organisation at the disposal of the [National Recruiting] Campaign   5
and further recommends the affiliated bodies to give all possible local support.

Quoted in David Boulton, *Objection Overruled,* **1967**

Questions

1   What domestic and international arguments are put forward in extracts **1.6**, **1.7** and **1.8** against involvement in the war? Assess their validity.
2   What commitments are being made in **1.9** and **1.10**? To what extent can these be seen to be against the interests of Labour?
3   What is mean by 'affiliated bodies' [**1.10, line 6**]?
4   What evidence is there in these extracts of a split between the ILP element and the other groups which made up the Labour Party? You might find it helpful to discuss the different ways of becoming a member of the Labour Party. (Only the ILP had local groups which made individual membership possible.)
5   With reference to your wider reading, how accurate is the picture given in **1.7** of the attitude of German Socialists to the outbreak of war? Did the German working classes in fact resist the war effort in its early stages?

During the war, Labour was again torn over the questions of political truce, coalition and conscription. Yet the Labour Party emerged from the First World War with a new structure, and sufficiently united to function efficiently as a major political party.

By 28 August 1914, a political truce had been formalised. A group, which included Arthur Henderson, newly appointed Chairman of the Parliamentary Labour Party, agreed that until January 1915 there would be no contested elections for vacant seats. The government's need for this is a sign of the Labour Party's growing significance: they had, after all, never put up more than 78 candidates. In February 1915 the truce was negotiated, and it was agreed that there would be discussions between the three parties before any vacant seat was filled; in other words, the truce would be tried out each time. The effect of this limited arrangement was that there were virtually no contests until, in January 1918, a Labour Party Conference carried the motion that 'the political truce should no longer be recognised'.

The extraordinary fact is that, despite the deeply divisive views put forward in the first few months of the war, the Labour Party held together. Ramsay MacDonald resigned as Chairman of the Parliamentary Party to be replaced by Arthur Henderson in August 1914, but he remained on the Labour Party Executive as representative of the ILP and thus there was never a complete schism between the pro- and anti-war groups. Even the appointment of Labour men (Henderson, Hodges, Barnes) to the coalition governments did not inflict permanent damage on the Party, and in the last two years of the war, the various groups came together to plan the future, regardless of earlier divisions over industrial disputes, pacificism and conscription.

Adelman[3] suggests that the Russian Revolution of March 1917 is the key to the restoration of Party unity. Henderson visited Russia for six weeks and was anxious to send a British delegation to the Stockholm Conference (1917) of belligerent nations' socialists. The Labour Party Conference of August 1917 voted in favour of this by a huge majority; a powerful and hostile press campaign reduced, but failed to remove, the majority at a second vote, so the Prime Minister stepped in. Given the choice of resigning from the Cabinet or resigning as Secretary of the Labour Party, Henderson left the Cabinet, and the Party now concentrated on its war aims and plans for the future. Opposition to the war became increasingly respectable. At home, the heroic soldier–poet, Sassoon, had rejected the war; abroad the Bolsheviks published secret treaties which seemed to confirm socialist convictions that the war had been one of imperialist aggression. The war aims agreed at the Party Conference of December 1917 explicitly rejected imperialism and demanded, not just control by legislatures of Foreign Policy but also recognition of a supranational authority, or League of Nations.

The Party also began to plan its own future. In January and February of 1918, the new constitution of the Labour Party set it on the path to future power, by broadening its base, and by aiming it clearly at a socialist future.

All workers by hand and brain, whether trade unionists or not, could now form local parties, and these would be represented by five seats on the National Executive. The aim of the Labour Party was:

1.11

> To secure for the producers by hand or brain the full fruits of their industry and the most equitable distribution thereof that may be possible upon the basis of the common ownership of the means of production and the best obtainable system of popular administration and control of each industry or service.

5

Clause IV, Labour Party Constitution, 1918

Questions

1   With reference to **1.11**,
   (i) what specific commitment is made for the future of British industry?
   (ii) what development during the war had encouraged Labour to hope for these changes?
2   Discuss the 'tone' of the Clause [**1.11**]. What factors help to explain its lack of militancy at this stage of the war?

The end of the war came too soon for the new structure to show itself to advantage at the General Election of December 1918. Nonetheless, there was clear evidence that Labour had survived the divisions of the war and was set to be the second major party in British politics. In December 1918, out of 11 million votes cast, Labour gained 2 million votes (and 63 seats). This appears limited, given that 388 candidates had stood, but it compares well with the 28 seats gained by the Asquith Liberals, and with the 42 seats and less than half million votes Labour had achieved in December 1910. Between 1918 and 1922 Labour won 14 by-elections and at the 1922 election Labour won 142 seats. The Labour Party had arrived, though whether the reorganisation, the rejection of

Communism and the readiness to accommodate different views within one party would have happened without the war is hard to assess.

The Liberal Party: death and dismemberment?

There is similar controversy about the 'end' of the Liberal Party; about the conduct of the war by the two Prime Ministers, Asquith and Lloyd George; and about the conflict between them. There are no Cabinet papers for most of the First World War, and so evidence must come from more personal memoirs and letters, and from parliamentary records. It is interesting to note that both Asquith and Lloyd George had female confidants: Lloyd George's secretary, Frances Stevenson, clearly knew a great deal more than the typical secretary should; and Asquith wrote almost daily to Venetia Stanley, the daughter of Lord Sheffield, who was 27 years old in 1914.

The Liberals had been in power since 1905, and although their majority of 1906 had been much reduced, and they had not won many by-elections since 1910, they had survived the challenges of the Suffragettes, of The Irish Question and of industrial unrest. The Cabinet had remained unchanged for some time, and even disagreements about its attitudes to the impending war had failed to break up Asquith's Cabinet.

The diaries of Charles Hobhouse provide much 'inside information' for this period.

1.12   Discussions in Cabinet, 2 August 1914

> The PM, Haldane and I [were] for war if there were even a merely
> technical breach of the Belgium Treaty. Pease and Runciman were
> strongly against war but not for unconditional neutrality. Burns on
> Sunday morning was saying this meant either unconditional neutra-
> lity or (leaning over the table shaking his clenched fists) war with   5
> both hands, naval and military. He was interrupted by McK and
> LLG saying 'but which is your policy?' He hesitated, they repeated
> the challenge, and with a gulp said 'Neutrality under circumstance'
> and turned very white. John Morley then said, 'You all know my
> views, those of a lifetime, I cannot renounce, and if you persevere in   10
> intervention, I cannot return to this room.' As he said the same thing
> about once a month for three years, no-one took this very seriously.
> At the end of our meeting, JB lent forward and in a few words of
> deep feeling said he must separate himself from his colleagues with
> whom he had served in friendship for nine years and from a PM he   15

loved. He was moved to tears. J Morley said he too could not continue.

From the diaries of Charles Hobhouse, in E. David (ed.),
Inside Asquith's Cabinet, **1977**

Hobhouse also gives an interesting picture of how unity in this diverse Cabinet was maintained by Asquith, and his views of Lloyd George.

1.13   23 March 1915

We sit round the table thus: Asquith, Harcourt, Beauchamp, Montagu, Emmott, Simon, Birrell, Pease, Samuel, Haldane, Grey, opposite the PM, George, Crewe, McKenna, Runciman, Hobhouse, Lucas, Wood, Churchill, Kitchener.

The PM's abilities are as transcendent as ever: his qualities more   5
noticeable. Temper, tact, courage quite marvellous. Some of us think he is a little too considerate to the Opposition, but it is a wise fault.
. . . LLG is in council as in every other relation wonderfully versatile, adroit and quick with an unrivalled, indeed miraculous power of picking other people's brains. He reads and educates himself conti-   10
nuously but is contemptible as an administrator and his want of knowledge of money values has cost us quite as much as his audacity and resource have gained. He is fickle, ungrateful, untruthful, but not, I think, envious, and quite appreciative of others' abilities.

From the diaries of Charles Hobhouse, in E. David (ed.), *Inside Asquith's Cabinet*, **1977**

Montagu described what he thought of Lloyd George in a letter to Asquith dated May 1914:

1.14

To work with him [Lloyd George] is a revelation of rare and marvellous qualities of enthusiasm, of courage, and of industry, and also of directed ambition. I used to think he was out for popularity: that is quite untrue. He will do nothing for popularity which he believes to be unsound . . . I believe him to be perfectly honest when he says, as   5
he frequently does, that he never wishes to be Prime Minister. He wants to control the machine, and the policy of the machine, but he

recognises his own limitations. He has a reverence and a loyalty for
you, and if the Party would let him, I think they would find genui-
nely that he would rather serve under almost anybody, provided he   10
could be secured in the second place. He has never made any disguise
of the fact to me that the Treasury is the wrong place for him. He
feels, as every critic must feel, that his genius is not for departmental
work, or for the details of complicated Acts of Parliament. He recognises that the position of the Chancellor of the Exchequer is such   15
that he could not get his way if another man was Chancellor, nor
could he claim his coveted second place; but he hates the routine
work, he loves big splashes of colour and particular principles.

Quoted in C. Hazlehurst, *Politicians at War, July 1914–May 1915*,
1971

Questions

1   What are the different attitudes to the impending war expressed by
     the Cabinet in **1.12**? Which of them did in fact resign at the outbreak
     of war?
2   With reference to **1.12** and your wider reading,
     (i) identify the Cabinet positions held by the different Cabinet mem-
         bers referred to by Hobhouse (they were politicians who had
         been in power for some time).
     (ii) about which of these people does Hobhouse make his feelings
         clear? To whom is he sympathetic or unsympathetic?
3   (i) What adverse comments are made by both Hobhouse [**1.13**] and
         Montagu [**1.14**] about Lloyd George?
     (ii) What strong points does each see in him?
4   How useful and reliable do you consider these views in **1.13** and **1.14**
     to be? How are your perceptions affected by the knowledge that
     Lloyd George was in fact to become Prime Minister?

The formation of the Coalition

The reasons why an apparently secure and united government was
replaced by a Coalition under Asquith has been the subject of much
debate among historians. Beaverbrook began the discussion in his
account published in 1922, claiming that it was the resignation of Fisher
over the use of the navy in the Dardanelles in 1915 which precipitated
the change. Trevor Wilson[4] argues that Fisher could have been replaced
without the restructuring; but Churchill thought Fisher was mad in the
way he reacted; and Fisher commented to Balfour (5 June 1915) that

'it was better to wreck the government than the navy'. Stephen Koss[5] however, prefers a conspiracy theory: Churchill visited France on 8 and 9 May, and spoke to Colonel Repington. On 14 May, Repington's despatch [concerning the munitions crisis] was published in *The Times*, and on 19 May 1915, the Coalition was formed. Hazlehurst[6] rejects this picturesque interpretation, arguing that Asquith had 'long appreciated' that Coalition might be necessary and so saw the double crisis as the perfect moment. Hazlehurst also points out that, by persuading the Commons to accept the new Ministry without the requirement to re-elect the members concerned, Asquith avoided the General Election which would otherwise have been due in January 1916, under the 1911 Parliament Act, and which might have proved damaging to the Party as well as to the government. The following extracts throw some light on the establishment of the Coalition:

1.15   12 May 1915, Mr Booth (Liberal MP for Pontefract) asked Asquith:

Whether in view of the present war and in view of the steps necessary to be taken in order to grapple with the rearrangement of industry and social life consequent upon a prolonged struggle, he will consider the desirability of admitting into the ranks of ministers leading members of the various political parties in this House.   5
[Asquith in reply said that Coalition was 'not in contemplation'.]

Hansard, Vol 71, col 1642

1.16   Debate on the Whitsuntide adjournment, 19 May 1915

Mr Asquith: Owing to another engagement which I could not put off, I was unable to make this motion myself for the adjournment, but I think it right, at the earliest possible moment, to say two or three words to the House in regard to the matters which have been the subject of public report and rumour. I cannot say more at the   5
moment than that steps are in contemplation which involve the reconstruction of the government on a broader personal and political basis. Nothing is yet definitely arranged, but to avoid any possible misapprehension, and as the House is about to adjourn, I wish here and now to make clear to everybody three things.   10
   The first is that any change that takes place will not affect the offices of the Head of Government or of the Secretary of State for Foreign Affairs. They will continue to be held as they are now. The

second is, that there is absolutely no change of any kind in contemplation in the policy of the country in regard to the continued   15
prosecution of the war with every possible energy and by means of
every available resource.

The third and last point, one of great importance to my Honourable friends behind me, and I have no doubt also to the Honourable
Gentlemen who sit behind the Leader of the Opposition, is this: any   20
reconstruction that may be made will be for the purposes of the war
alone and is not to be taken in any other quarter as any reason for
indicating anything in the nature of surrender or compromise on the
part of any person or body of persons of their several political
purposes and ideals . . .   25

Mr Bonar Law: I think it only necessary to say on behalf of my
friends and myself that at the stage which this matter has reached,
our sole consideration, taking into account what further steps will be
taken, will be the sole idea as to what is the best method of finishing
the war successfully – and we shall leave out of our minds absolutely   30
all considerations, political or otherwise, beyond the war. Of course,
if such an arrangement should take place, it is obvious that our
convictions on other subjects will remain unchanged and will be
settled when this danger is over.

Hansard, Vol 71, col 2392–2393

1.17   Motion proposed by Sir John Simon, 3 June 1915

That leave be given to introduce a bill to make temporary provision
for rendering unnecessary the re-election of members of the House of
Commons on acceptance of office.

Hansard, Vol 77, col 14

Questions

1   For what reasons did Mr Booth recommend a Coalition [**1.15**]?
     Assess the validity of these reasons.
2   What anxieties is Asquith trying to allay in **1.16**?
3   What problems do you find in dealing with the 'parliamentary' style
     of Asquith's and Bonar Law's comments [**1.16**]? How do you explain
     the complex and yet vague manner of speech used? (You might
     compare these statements to statements by modern Prime Ministers
     and Leaders of the Opposition.)

4   Taking these extracts [1.15–1.17] and their dates together, do you think that the House of Commons would feel it had been adequately informed and consulted about what was happening in government?

5   Explain why Sir John Simon's motion [1.17] was necessary, and why the government would have been anxious for it to be carried.

The new Coalition Cabinet was not united on every issue, and the 'convictions on other subjects' referred to by Bonar Law in 1.16 frequently surfaced. Hobhouse was one of those who was excluded from the new Coalition Cabinet, but he gives an 'interesting' account of 'Cabinet discord', which contrasts with the more peaceful Cabinets he had sat through:

1.18   14 October 1915

I saw WR [Walter Runciman]. He gave an interesting picture of Cabinet discord. Lansdowne, Curzon, Law, A. Chamberlain were for leaving the Cabinet if conscription were not proposed. Law chiefly because the Gallipoli peninsula was not abandoned and Chamberlain because of his position as reversionary leader. Curzon   5
qualified his desire to resign by a declaration that in that event his criticism would be confined to any subject of actual disagreement. Balfour and Long would remain in whatever happened to carry on the government, AJB being against and Long for compulsory service. With them would go Churchill who was pining to get abroad to the   10
Dardanelles and LLG who saw no opening to a leadership and was much afraid that he had muddled the Ministry of Munitions for which he would be called to account and thought he had better get out of harness while there was yet time to throw the blame on someone else. The PM was still a convinced voluntaryist but equally   15
determined on keeping the government together ... McKenna who was the PM's only confidant was determined to resign as was WR and these two thought Loulou [Harcourt] would also go if conscription was carried in Cabinet. K had been won over and had told the Cabinet he wanted 35,000 men a week whereas his departmental   20
people had only asked for 30,000. Simon, characteristically, could only express his determination to stand by the PM. Henderson had a violent altercation with LLG and told him and the Cabinet squarely that Labour would resist conscription by every means in and out of Parliament.   25

From the diaries of Charles Hobhouse, in E. David (ed.),
***Inside Asquith's Cabinet*, 1977**

Questions

1   Using the information in **1.18**,
     (i) show to what extent the splits within the Cabinet ran along the
     lines of party.
     (ii) What issues other than conscription were identified by Runciman
     as being likely to lead to resignations?
2   What allowances do you think should be made for the 'hearsay'
     nature of **1.18** as compared to Hobhouse's other accounts, such as
     1.12 and **1.13**?

Despite Runciman's predictions, Asquith's Coalition lasted for another
year. Conscription was introduced without fragmenting the Cabinet, and
when Asquith was replaced by Lloyd George's Coalition, the key issue
was confidence in Asquith, rather than any single controversy.

Some historians, such as P. Scally,[7] have seen the formation of Lloyd
George's government as the result of years of planning. Back in 1910 in
Criccieth, Lloyd George had produced a memorandum arguing in favour
of a permanent coalition government for social peace. But in December
1916, more immediate constraints brought about the change in
leadership.

There had been rumours of a 'conspiracy' to 'unload' Asquith as early
as March 1915. Asquith, in a letter to Venetia Stanley on 29 March
1915, wrote:

1.19

Northcliffe (for some unknown reason) has been engineering a campaign to supplant me by LLG. McK of course quite certain that
LLG and perhaps Winston are 'in it'. Which I don't believe.

Quoted in Stephen Koss, *Asquith*, 1976

1.20   Frances Stevenson noted in her diary for 8 April 1915:

C [i.e. Lloyd George] was also bothered last week by a conspiracy
against the PM . . . side by side with this was another tale, that there
would be a Coalition government and C's name was coupled with
Balfour's in connection with this. C was very upset as this was the
last thing he would wish for and also he could see that the PM was   5
rather suspicious of him as the rumour must have come from some-

where. C went to have a talk with the PM about it and found the old boy in tears.

A. J. P. Taylor (ed.), *Lloyd George: A Diary by Frances Stevenson*, 1917

Here is Asquith's account of the same meeting:

1.21

As for himself he [Lloyd George] declared that he owed everything to me, that I had stuck to him and protected him and defended him even when every man's hand was against him and that he would rather (1) break stones (2) dig potatoes (3) be hung and quartered (these were all metaphors used at different stages of his broken but   5
impassioned harangue) than do an act or say a word or harbour a thought that was disloyal to me and he said that every one of his colleagues felt the same. His eyes were wet with tears and I am sure that with all his Celtic capacity for impulsive and momentary fervour he was quite sincere. Of course I assured him that I had never for a   10
moment doubted him, which is quite true, and he warmly wrung my hand and abruptly left the room.

H. H. Asquith, *Memories and Reflections*, Vol 2, 1928

Questions

1   Compare these accounts [1.19–1.21] of the same rumour. Who is blamed for the rumour?
2   What were the later links between Northcliffe and Lloyd George to be?
3   How significant is it that Asquith is reporting some years after the event? Do you think his account is at all coloured by what happened in December 1916 and later? Why?

By mid-1916 many people felt that Asquith had ceased to be effective. He was said to drink heavily; his son Raymond was killed in the trenches and he visibly found this a hard blow from which to recover. Sir Henry Wilson, Officer Commanding IV Corps in France, made his feelings clear, both in his diary, and in letters to the Liberal, Lord Milner.

1.22   Diary of Sir Henry Wilson, 30 January 1916

From my visit home, it is clear to me that so long as we keep Asquith
as PM we shall never go to war. And this is a most dangerous thing.
He will do nothing himself and will not allow anyone else to do
anything.

Quoted in R. J. Scally, *Origins of the Lloyd George Coalition*, 1975

1.23   Letter to Milner, 4 April 1916

There will be an absolute howl and yell of delight through the whole
army the day Squiff falls and an amazing warmth and belief in those
I have mentioned [Milner, DLG, Carson, and 'one Labour man
added'] when they take over and GOVERN.

Quoted in R. J. Scally, *Origins of the Lloyd George Coalition*, 1975

1.24   Letter to Milner, 20 April 1916

If ever a man deserved to be tried and shot that man is the PM.
There is a volume of feeling vs him and his miserable crowd, rising
out here amongst the soldiers of all ranks which delights me . . . we
hope that you and Carson and LLG have at last got him by the
throat. NO MERCY PLEASE.   5

Quoted in R. J. Scally, *The Origins of the Lloyd George Coalition*, 1975

Questions

1   What complaints does Wilson make about Asquith [**1.22–1.24**]? How
     far were they justified by the actual conduct of the war to date?
2   (i) Comment on the tone of these extracts [**1.22–1.24**]. How does the
     fact that they are personal, and privately expressed views affect
     their validity?
     (ii) Compare these comments with Hobhouse's earlier evaluation of
     Asquith as Prime Minister [**1.13**]. What factors might explain the
     differences in these opinions?
3   Discuss the probability that Wilson would be an accurate source for
     'the soldiers of all ranks' and their opinions.[8]

The formation of Lloyd George's Coalition on 7 December 1916 changed the conduct of the war; it also changed forever the history of the Liberal Party. From its formation to the end of the war, Asquith mostly avoided confrontation with the new government. The exception is the so-called Maurice Debate of 9 May 1918. The circumstances are well known: General Maurice's allegations of a shortage of reinforcements caused Asquith to ask for a Select Committee to enquire into the problem. The Motion asking for the Select Committee was received as a vote of no confidence in the government, and marked the final split in the Liberal Party. It certainly confirmed the dominance of Lloyd George, and it has often been claimed that the voting patterns in the Maurice Debate are the key to the issuing of 'coupons' (the endorsement of candidates approved by the Coalition to distinguish them from Asquithian Liberals) for the election of December 1918. In fact, as demonstrated by Trevor Wilson[9] the 'Maurice' votes do not tally with the coupons. Of the 159 couponed Liberals, only 54 had actually gone into the government lobby in the debate. Some had abstained, or had been absent, or were not MPs at the time; but 11 couponed candidates were people who had actually voted against the government, including Josiah Wedgwood, who had said in the debate 'I have very little confidence indeed in the present government and I think that a change would be extremely desirable'.

No change had happened in May 1918 and, despite the withdrawal of Labour to fight their own campaign, Lloyd George was able to take his Coalition into peace, thus providing yet one more interesting contrast with events at the end of the Second World War. But Lloyd George's survival in power confirmed the end of his Party, which had seemed both strong and permanent in 1914.

References

1   Lord Curzon, in a letter to Lord Lamington, 22 August 1914, in *Life of Lord Curzon*, Vol 3, by the Rt Hon the Earl of Ronaldshay, Ernest Benn, 1928, pp. 121–2

2   R. Blake, *The Conservative Party from Peel to Thatcher*, Fontana, 1985, pp. 195–7

3   P. Adelman, *The Rise of the Labour Party*, Longman, 1972

4   T. Wilson, 'The Coupon and the General Election of 1918', in *Journal of Modern History*, XXXVI, 1964

5   S. Koss, *Asquith*, Allen Lane, 1976

6   C. Hazlehurst, *Politicians at War*, Cape, 1971

7   P. Scally, *The Origins of the Lloyd George Coalition*, Princeton, 1975

8   The following sources may help with this question:
     G. Coppard, *With a Machine Gun to Cambrai*, HMSO, 1969
     P. Vansittart, *Voices from the Great War*, Cape, 1981
     D. Winter, *Death's Men*, Allen Lane, 1978

9   T. Wilson, 'The Coupon and the General Election of 1918' in *Journal of Modern History*, XXXVI, 1964

2 The economy and the First World War

War economy

The First World War is probably the first occasion on which a whole economic system was transformed to meet the needs of a military struggle. The term 'war economy' is defined by A. Milward, *Economic Effects of the Two World Wars in Britain*, which is a very detailed study of the transformation which took place. Extract **2.1** gives the reader a chance to assess Milward's definition, as a starting point for consideration of economic developments in the war years.

2.1

> The aim was to win, ... no matter what the cost. Therefore the main
> economic priority was to produce the necessary quantity of goods to
> defeat the enemy. Consequently the ultimate economic purpose was
> quite different from that of peacetime and the kind of economy which
> was created has come to be known loosely by the term 'war econ-   5
> omy'. The term is a loose one, for it is a matter of historical fact that
> most of the 'war economies' which have existed have neither had
> such simple priorities as, nor much resemblance to, the war econo-
> mies which existed in Britain. It may even be questioned whether
> historians have not exaggerated the degree of unanimity of purpose   10
> which informed the economy of Britain during the two world wars.
> Nevertheless it must be stated that it is a matter of almost universal
> agreement that the British nation twice bent its united energies to
> creating an economy whose dominating purpose was to defeat the
> enemy, sweeping aside, gradually in the First World War, and almost   15
> from the beginning in the Second, most other claims on that
> economy.

A. S. Milward, *The Economic Effects of the Two World Wars on Britain*, 1984

Questions

1   Using the information in **2.1**, provide your own definition of a 'war economy'.
2   How do the aims of a war economy differ from those of a peacetime economy?
3   Consider the types of evidence which would be required to demonstrate the truth, or otherwise, of the comment that the British nation 'bent its united energies' to the creation of a war economy.

Changes in the economy

The rest of this chapter focuses on some aspects of economic change in Britain, in an attempt to decide on their extent and permanence or otherwise. One of the key areas of change and of the new methods of organisation was the Munitions Industry. The information on p. 32 summarises the progress by April 1917.

Questions

1   Find examples of 'military' vocabulary used to express civilian activity on **2.2**. What reasons can you suggest for using this kind of vocabulary?
2   Identify the various different starting points, or bases, used for the comparisons on this poster. How do these affect the statistical usefulness of the information offered?
3   Make a table to show the different levels of, and measures of success shown in **2.2**.
4   For what political reason might the year 1915, and specifically May 1915 (see BOMBS) be used as the base for **2.2**?
5   What do you see as the purpose of such a poster? At whom was it directed? Which groups are specifically encouraged to 'do more' here?

You might notice the omission from the poster of any mention of 'tanks'. These only came into mass use as the poster went into production. Aircraft too, which were beginning to be mass produced by 1917, are not included. By the end of the war, 52,027 military aircraft had been produced – nearly half the total military aircraft production of the Second World War.

One reason for the high production figures on the poster was the comparative peace on the industrial relations front. The dilution agreements (Extracts **2.3–2.6**) did boost production, and they were the subject of constant discussion and revision.

THE WAR OF MUNITIONS

HOW GREAT BRITAIN HAS MOBILISED HER INDUSTRIES

Since the outbreak of war in August 1914, Great Britain has grappled with the task of munitionment with astonishing success, and today she is one great Arsenal. Not only has she maintained her armies at the Front with ever-increasing supplies, but she has also materially assisted in the munitioning of her Allies. Despite the fact that more than five million men have been drafted to the Colours, she has raised a vast industrial army which is ceaselessly engaged upon the production of munitions. Her industries have been mobilised and placed upon a war footing, countless new factories have been erected, many old factories have been adapted for war purposes, and the output of munitions in the British Isles has been enormously increased. The workshops of Britain are at war, and they will know no truce till victory is secure.

WAR WORKERS There are two and a half million persons engaged on government work in Munition trades, of whom nearly half a million are women.

BOMBS Between May 1915 and December 1916, the output of Bombs was increased 33-fold.

NATIONAL PROJECTILE FACTORIES The New National Projectile Factories, which consist of bays of an average breadth of 40 feet, and a total length of 15 miles, are equipped with more than 10,000 machine tools, driven by 17 miles of shafting with an energy of 25,000 horse-power. The weekly output of this group of factories alone amounts to more than 10,000 tons weight of projectiles.

MACHINE GUNS The number of Machine Guns available for the British Army is now twenty times as great as it was at the end of the first year of the War.

TRAINING SCHOOLS Up to December 1916, over 26,000 students had passed through Munition Training Schools, and at least 21,000 had been placed in employment.

GUN AMMUNITION The total amount of Shell produced during the first year of the War is now being produced in the following periods:–
Field Gun and Howitzer Shell
– About 8 days
Medium Gun and Howitzer Shell
– About 5 days
Heavy Gun and Howitzer Shell
– About 1 day

HIGH EXPLOSIVES In High Explosives, the production is now more than 100 times what it was in January 1915.

THE ARMY In 1914 the British Army numbered 275,000. Since the outbreak of war more than five million men have been enrolled in the forces of the Crown.

HEAVY GUNS The monthly output of Heavy Guns during 1916 was more than ten times what it was during 1915.

WOMEN IN INDUSTRY Of the 500 different processes in munition work, upon which women are engaged, two-thirds had never been performed by a woman previously to a year ago.

NATIONAL ARSENALS Before the War there were three National Arsenals working for the land service; today there are more than 100.

THE NAVY To equip a sailor takes nearly eight times as many workmen as are required to provide a soldier with all he needs in the way of munitions. Since the outbreak of war the personnel of the British Navy has increased from 146,000 to 350,000.

◄—2.2   **Information derived from the poster:** *The War of Munitions: How Great Britain has mobilised her industries*, **April 1917**

2.3

Alterations in working conditions

Schedule II, paragraph 7 provides: 'Due notice shall be given to the workmen concerned wherever practicable of any changes of working conditions which it is desired to introduce as the result of the establishment becoming a controlled establishment, and opportunity   5
for local consultation with workmen or their representatives shall be given if desired.'

Procedure:

1   The workmen in the shop in which a change is to be made should
    be requested by the employer to appoint a deputation of their   10
number together with their local Trade Union Representative if they desire, to whom particulars of the proposed change could be explained.

2   At the interview, the employer, after explaining the change pro-
    posed and giving the date when it is to come into operation,   15
should give the deputation full opportunity of raising any points they desire in connection therewith, so that if possible the introduction may be made with the consent of all Parties.

3   Should the deputation be unable at the interview to concur in the
    change, opportunity should be given for further local consultation,   20
when representatives of the Trade Unions concerned might be present.

Notes on the dilution of skilled labour, prepared by the Munitions Labour Supply Committee for Guidance of Controlled Establishments (Cir L6), October 1915

2.4   **From Frances Stevenson's Diary, 1 February 1916**

Today the men from Lang's on the Clyde are out on strike owing to the introduction of women into the works. Mrs Drummond (WSPU) came to see me yesterday on the subject of holding meetings up there to try and make the men see the criminality of their actions.

A. J. P. Taylor (ed.), *Lloyd George: a Diary by Frances Stevenson*, 1971

2.5

A great step forward has been taken at the Parkhead works, Glasgow.
The employers have agreed that the same rates are to be paid to
women as to men.

The Woman Worker Magazine, **March 1916**

**2.6   Directions relating to the employment and remuneration of
semi-skilled and unskilled men on munitions work of a class which
prior to the war was customarily undertaken by skilled labour.**

(Note – these directions are strictly confined to the war period and are
subject to the observance of Schedule II of the Munitions of War
Act, 1914)

General

1   Operations on which skilled men are at present employed, but   5
which by reason of their character can be performed by semi-skilled
or unskilled labour, may be done by such labour during the period of
war.

2   Where semi-skilled or unskilled male labour is employed on work
identical with that customarily undertaken by skilled labour, the   10
time rates and piece prices and premium bonus times shall be the
same as customarily obtained for the operations when performed by
skilled labour.

3   Where skilled men are at present employed they shall not be
displaced by less skilled labour unless other skilled employment is   15
offered to them there or elsewhere.

4   Piecework prices and premium bonus time allowances, after they
have been established, shall not be altered unless the means or
methods or manufacture are changed.

5   Overtime, night shift, Sunday and holiday allowances shall be   20
paid to such machinemen on the same basis as to skilled men.

**Order No 71, 24 January 1917; Order No 667, 26 June 1917. Quoted in
R. W. Breach and R. M. Hartwell, *British Economy and Society*,
1870–1970, 1972**

Questions

1 The 'Notes for Guidance' [2.3] suggest a very cautious approach to the workforce. Suggest reasons for this moderate procedure.

2 What evidence is there in 2.3 that Trade Unions played a smaller role in this period than they were to later?

3 (i) Using the information from extract 2.6, attempt a definition of 'dilution of labour'.

   (ii) What safeguards were offered to skilled men in 2.6 (in terms of their security and of the duration of the dilution)?

   (iii) How far is it accurate to say that semi–skilled and unskilled workers did very well out of these agreements [2.3 and 2.6]? Quote details to support your answer.

4 What is implied about women in point 2 of 2.6? Compare the two brief extracts [2.4 and 2.5]. (The question of women will be referred to further in Chapter 3.)

The Trade Unions were prepared to accept dilution of labour, and even women workers, partly at least because the cost of living was remaining at an acceptable level and because some of their long-term economic and social aims appeared to be being conceded. The railways were 'rented' by the government, and operated as one system, under an Act of Parliament of 1871, which allowed them to be taken over in time of war; the coal industries were effectively nationalised after the South Wales strikes of July 1915; ocean-going vessels followed, after public outcry at the huge profits being made. Food prices were controlled and rationing inevitably followed, seen by some as fulfilling the socialist maxim 'to each according to his need'. Before the war, welfare developments had begun to shelter the people from economic hardship (National Insurance, Maternity Benefit, Old Age Pensions). During the war these provisions were joined by family allowances for serving men, free milk and food for infants and nursing mothers, free school meals higher up the age range and so on. Incomes were improved by high levels of overtime, and by the earnings of the 1,600,000 women newly in employment, as well as the old and young entering employment to replace the 6,100,000 men in the services.

On the other hand, many wartime developments were very inflation-ary, or went against the free trade principles to which Britain adhered.

This chapter makes no attempt to write the full statistical history of the war, but on p. 36 are a few figures to consider. They have been put into tabular form for more direct comparison. You may wish to use the questions as a basis for discussion in class; they may also profitably be compared with 6.3–6.7.

2.7 Various statistics on the war years:

Treasury Notes in circulation

A	Year	Value (in £)
	Dec 1914	33,719,000
	Dec 1915	88,598,000
	Dec 1920	353,358,000

B	Year	Exports (in £ millions)	Imports (in £ millions)	Balance of payments deficit (in £ millions)
	1914	526	696	170
	1915	483	850	367
	1918	532	1,316	783.9

C	Year	Income tax	Excess profits tax
	1914	1s 2d*	—
	1915–16	3s 0d	50%
	1917–18	6s 0d	80%

* Amounts in shillings (s) and pence (d); 12d = 1s (5 new pence); 20s = £1 (100 new pence)

D *Expenditure on the war*
Total expenditure: £9,593 million
28% met by taxation
72% met by borrowing: £850 million from USA
remaining £5,000 million (approx.) met by selling assets abroad and by national borrowing

E *Farming and prices*
By 1918, 3 million more acres were being farmed than in 1914.
Corn Production Act 1917 fixed minimum prices and allowed for subsidies to extend production.

Derived from information in Breach and Hartwell, *British Economy and Society, 1870–1970*, 1972; and A. S. Milward, *The Economic Effects of the Two World Wars on Britain*, 1984

Questions

1   What is the significance of the figures in **2.7** (A)? How do they reveal the damaging effect of the war on the British financial system?
2   What reasons can you suggest for the figures in **2.7** (B)? What commodities would be likely to have been imported?
3   (i) What are the likely post-war effects of **2.7** (C) and **2.7** (D)?
    (ii) Show how these figures illustrate Britain's reliance on the USA.
    (iii) What do you know of the USA's attitude to these figures, and of their impact on international affairs generally?
4   In the years before the war, the question of 'Protection' for farming had been a major political issue. Explain clearly how **2.7** (E) represents a major shift in policy for the Liberals in the government.
5   How far do these figures in **2.7** confirm or refute the concept of the 'war economy' as defined in **2.1**? Justify your answer.

At the end of the war, almost all the 'socialist' machinery of the war was undone; the Ministry of Reconstruction had planned to maintain some of it, but parliamentary opinion was against it. The Coupon Election had produced 'The wealthiest, the least intelligent and the least representative House of Commons since Waterloo.'[1]

Lloyd George was not able to behave as the Tories had after Waterloo, when the reactionary government of Lord Liverpool suppressed political demonstrations with violence, and protected the wealthy land owners with a Corn Law which raised the price of bread. The enfranchisement of the labouring classes (borough constituencies 1867; county constituencies 1884) meant that the government could no longer risk ignoring poverty, starvation and mass unemployment simply for the benefit of the middle class managers and owners of industry. There were high tax increases in 1919, and desperate action was taken in 1925 to deal with the excess of paper money; both these measures affected the rich as well as the poor. It had been intended to keep agricultural prices high by the Agricultural Act of 1920 (like the Corn Laws of 1815) but this was repealed in 1921. The working classes were not happy with the return to pre-war methods and rates – in 1919, 35 million working days were lost through strikes; in 1920 the figure was 27 million working days. On the other hand, the wealthy were not able to point to enormous benefits as restrictions were removed.

The limited taste of state control which Britain experienced during the First World War served as a basis for discussion throughout the years up to the Second World War. Here are two extracts commenting on its usefulness:

2.8

I am disinclined to admit that all the measures of industrial and
commercial organisations adopted during the war which are com-
monly lumped together under the term State Control were merely
necessary evils to be got rid of as soon as possible and never to be
thought about again. A considerable extension of co-operative and   5
collective enterprise seems to me probable and desirable in time of
peace, and I believe that there is something to be learnt from the
experiments in State Control during the war which may be of positive value in the difficult times ahead.

E. M. H. Lloyd, in the Preface to *Experiments in State Control*, **the
Carnegie Endowment for International Peace, 1924; quoted in A. S.
Milward,** *The Economic Effects of the Two World Wars on Britain*, **1984**

2.9

Totalitarian war can hardly anywhere stop short of socialism. There is
here an inequality of ideological sacrifice which cannot be avoided.
Those who want socialism in peace can find war in this respect to their
liking. Those who trust to individualism in peace must be ready to
surrender it in war. Private enterprise at private risk is a good ship,   5
and a ship that has brought us far, but it is a ship for fair weather
only.

William Beveridge, *Some Experiences of Economic Control in Wartime*,
1940

Questions

1   Summarise the arguments which Lloyd puts forward in favour of
     state control [**2.8**].
2   What are the 'difficult times' [**2.8, line 9**] of which Lloyd is writing?
     Was any attempt made to adopt 'state control' in the 1920s and
     1930s?
3   What does Beveridge mean by 'inequality of ideological sacrifice' [**2.9,
     line 2**]? Do you think he is right? Justify your answer.
4   How far do the sources quoted in this chapter support or refute the
     comments made by Beveridge?

In fact, the economy attempted to restore itself to 'normality' after the war, with the removal of the restrictions and regulations of wartime. But attitudes had been changed so that in the Second World War state interference in the economy occurred more rapidly and with far less opposition, and after 1945 there was to be much less feeling that things should revert to their pre-war condition. The First World War could be seen as a trial run for the much greater demands and controls of World War Two and beyond, controls which only came to be questioned – and lifted – in the 1980s. No-one at the time or since has claimed that the miseries of the post-war depression in the 1920s were entirely due either to the imposition of a war economy, or to its lifting; there were many other international and domestic factors which lie outside the scope of this brief survey.

Reference

1 P. Somervell, *The Reign of George V*, Faber, 1935

3 Society in the First World War

It is very easy to acquire, from contemporary novels and poetry in particular, a picture of a society transformed during the First World War. This picture may be made up of several attractive if impressionistic ingredients: women finally taking their proper place in society and working alongside the men; and a nation united against the common enemy, pulling together and sinking all personal and class differences in the greater struggle. Even the knowledge that such a society – if it ever existed – failed to survive into the 1920s, does not entirely dispel the illusion.

This book cannot begin to provide evidence on all aspects of society in the Great War; nor are there sources which allow close study of personal and social change, since it was not until the years just before the Second World War that governments became interested in the 'observation' of the people. Memoirs and diaries, among civilians at least, come predominantly from the 'educated classes'. Oral history archives, too, tend to accumulate the memories of the articulate, and often of those 'out of step' with the majority. For example, the Imperial War Museum's Oral History Archive has more interviews with Conscientious Objectors than with any other civilian category.

This chapter therefore offers instead a range of sources through three 'case histories' which, it is hoped, will stimulate discussion, and remind students of the risks of generalisation. These case histories concern women [3.1–3.3]; industrial disorder [3.4–3.6]; and some evidence about attitudes to anti-conscriptionists and Conscientious Objectors [3.7–3.15]. By considering the various sources offered for study in this chapter, it should be possible to estimate the extent to which British society was united in face of the German threat in the First World War. There was, after all, no serious threat of invasion as there was to be in 1940; Britain was more confident in its own strength than it was to be in the next war. On the other hand, from 1916 onwards, Britain experienced mass conscription for the first time in its history, and put its first mass army into the field. With these perspectives, it is interesting to consider, first, the question of the status and role of women.

3.1(a) Poster issued by the London County Council, February 1917

3.1(b)   Poster issued by the Women's National Land Service, 1917

Questions

1   What is the device used in **3.1(a)** to ensure that women feel that their work is directly related to the war?
2   (i) What other inducements are offered in **3.1(a)**?
     (ii) In what ways is the woman in **3.1(b)** apparently different from the one in **3.1(a)**?
3   How do you think that these posters may have helped recruitment for war work? (This can only be a matter for opinion and discussion, since there was no such thing as market research, or polling.)

For whatever reason, increasing numbers of women went to work in munitions factories. In November 1916, for example, 100 women worked at Woolwich Arsenal in London; a year later 30,000 women were employed there. But alongside this revolution in women's work, we need to consider the other familiar image of women in the First World War: that of the woman of leisure, recruiter and do-gooder.

3.2 Posters aimed at women of leisure

3.2(a)

TO THE
YOUNG WOMEN OF LONDON

Is your "Best Boy" wearing Khaki? If not don't **YOU THINK** he should be?

If he does not think that you and your country are worth fighting for—do you think he is **WORTHY** of you?

Don't pity the girl who is alone—her young man is probably a soldier—fighting for her and her country—and for **YOU**.

If your young man neglects his duty to his King and Country, the time may come when he will **NEGLECT YOU**.

Think it over—then ask him to

JOIN THE ARMY TO-DAY

Printed by David Allen & Sons Ltd. Harrow, London, etc.

3.2(b)

3.2(c)

TO DRESS EXTRAVAGANTLY IN WAR TIME IS WORSE THAN BAD FORM: IT IS UNPATRIOTIC

Published by the National War Savings Committee

3.2(d)

Eve is still Eve and she will always yearn after her 'frillies' because her man likes to see her keeping herself pretty for his return.

Women's Life, 16 November 1918

Questions

1 What date would you put to picture **3.2(a)**? Explain your answer.
2 Study **3.2(b)**, and discuss its probable target audience. How effective do you think it is likely to have been? Compare it to the stronger message of **3.2(a)**, **3.2(c)** and the brief extract from a women's magazine [**3.2(d)**].
3 Discuss the changes which in fact occurred during the war, both to women's clothes in general and to women's fashions.

Certain trivialising images of women may suggest that there was no serious change in the way women perceived themselves or were perceived. In some women's magazines, there was no sense at all that 'there's a war on', as people were to say in the next war. A visit to the British Library Newspaper Section at Colindale in North London, will provide the student with endless examples of features on cooking, fashion, marriage and child-care, without any reference to the war: a very different experience from that of reading magazines of the Second World War.

There were, of course, magazines which took a more determined line, and which might be seen as reflecting more accurately the true preoccupations of women in wartime. After all, 1,600,000 women were in paid employment during the war who had not been so before August 1914. *Modern Woman* was one such magazine and was attempting to deal with national issues. On p. 46 are three brief extracts.

3.3(a)

There is disappointment abroad, and at home, anger and recrimina-
tion. Minister is ready to give minister to the Dogs of War. Mr
Lloyd George, outspoken at last, stabs those of us who must remain
idle spectators of the struggle with his words 'too late'. What an
epitaph for any government. What a confession for a leader of men.   5

   Women are wage earners today and as such must be regarded as
having a direct interest in taxation. Whenever we buy our food, our
firewood, our coal, at enhanced prices we are assisting to pay Ministerial and Parliamentary salaries. We shall continue to pay, after the
war. Is it any wonder that we ask, are these men worth it?   10

Modern Woman, 1 January 1916

3.3(b)

It should be the woman's task to guard his wages for the man ...

   The Prime Minister, up to the moment of writing, is the only man
in England who has been compelled to do anything. Faced with the
choice of the introduction of a Bill for National Service or resignation, he chose National Service. The Prime Minister is over military   5
age.

Modern Woman, 15 January 1916

3.3(c)

What will become of the women when the men come home? By this
is meant the women who, regardless of fatigue, are working for their
country, either on the land or in the workshop. It is barely twelve
months since the great call arose for their services and already there
are those who would snatch well paid industry from the woman's   5
grasp and thrust her once again into those byways of sweated labour
from which the war has rescued her ...

   When the men come home, the women from long practice will be
semi-skilled and it is not the man who has known how to fight for
her in the trenches who will wish to thrust her from her well earned   10
place.

Modern Woman, 12 February 1916

Questions

1   What issues are being commented on in **3.3(a)** and **3.3(b)**? What threat is implied in **3.3(a)**? Why is it not relevant to discuss the threat of the ballot box?

2   What is the meaning of **3.3(c)**? How accurate a view do you think it gives of men's attitudes to women (compare what you have read in Chapter 2 and compare it also with the brief summary of figures which follows).

3   Discuss the 'tone' of these extracts [3.3(a)–(c)]. Do they seem to you to be 'typical' of women's magazine writing?

4   What kind of readers would a magazine like *Modern Woman* attract? Compare the possible audience to that which the posters earlier in this chapter were appealing to.

5   What are the risks, for a historian, of using this type of evidence? (Consider the limited readership and the main preoccupations of such magazines.)

Sources [3.1–3.3] show the difficulties confronting women as they tried to break the traditional mould. Comparison of the census figures of 1911 and 1921 confirm how very little progress was in fact made (some allowance must be made for changing classifications, though).

Number of women working

Occupation	1911	1921
Transport	27,000	72–75,000
Public Administration	105,000	668,000

The total number of women working increased by 234,000 out of a total population of 40 million. It is necessary to bear in mind, however, large losses in a number of traditional women's work areas, such as the clothing trade (where there were 200,000 *fewer* women workers), and domestic service. Thus, women hardly found their status, or even their self-perception transformed by war. Nor is it possible to find a nation wholly united, and burying its traditional divisions.

Industrial strife

Despite the Trade Union Truce at the beginning of the war, almost no month passed without some strike or dispute. Rather than reminding the reader of the famous events and personalities of 'Red Clydeside', this chapter offers some sources on the threatened national railway strike of August 1917.

3.4 Letter from the Chief Constable to the Home Office in Cardiff, 21 August 1917

> It seems apparent that although there is the usual strong disinclina-
> tion to become a Special Constable during times of labour unrest,
> yet, in this particular case, if the above strike should take place, it
> seems evident that there would be a good proportion of the industrial
> population which would be hostile to the strikers. Although these   5
> could not be relied upon to take any active part against the strikers,
> the police are of the opinion that they would at any rate preserve a
> benevolent neutrality towards the forces of law and order if the
> government were to step in and decide to run at any rate a limited
> train service protected by the military.   10

HO45/10884/346578

3.5 Notice posted by the Chief Constable of Staffordshire

> ## Defence of the Realm Act
> ### NOTICE
> THE CONTINUANCE OF TRAFFIC ON THE RAILWAYS IS NECESSARY FOR THE SAFETY OF THE NATION AND FOR THE PROSECUTION OF THE WAR. ANY PERSON WHO PREVENTS OR ATTEMPTS TO PREVENT ANOTHER PERSON FROM WORKING ON A RAILWAY AT THE PRESENT TIME IS LIABLE TO SIX MONTHS IMPRISONMENT.

HO45/10884/346578

Extracts from three newspapers for 21 August 1917:

3.6(a)

The Society (of Locomotive Engineers) has got itself into an unfortu-
nate position. Its leaders have chosen a critical time in the fortunes of
the country to prefer a demand for shortened hours. The reduction
for which they ask, not by any means unreasonable in ordinary times,
would be quite impossible to organise at a time when a large propor-   5
tion of engine drivers are at the front, and supplies of skilled labour
are difficult to obtain. The only effect of an eight hour day would in
fact be an increase in overtime.

Manchester Guardian, **21 August 1917**

3.6(b)

Here we are as a nation at the very crux of the war. It is preposterous
to suppose that some of the men upon whom we are relying to carry
us over the crux are going to fail us because they wish to make a
bargain in the height of the crisis. Their own women and children
would turn upon them if any action prolonged the agonies of our   5
brave wounded coming back all too slowly from the front and
increased the already too high price of food.

Daily Chronicle, **21 August 1917**

3.6(c)

This society, representing some 35,000 locomotive men, of whom
several thousand are serving in France – we should rather like to have
their opinion of its action – threatened to strike at twenty four hours
notice unless the principle of an eight hour day were conceded and
payment for overtime calculated at once on that basis.   5
   ... The truce that was entered into at the beginning of the war
debars them from raising any such fundamental points of railway
policy as they are attempting to bring forward. The National Union
of Railwaymen, with a membership of 400,000 is absolutely against
the stand taken by the Society of Locomotive Engineers and Fire-   10
men, and has denounced it through the mouth of its Secretary,
Mr J H Thomas MP as 'neither fair fighting nor common honesty'.

The Board of Trade meanwhile has 'proclaimed' the strike under the Munitions Act (1915) thus making it illegal to use the Society's funds for strike pay.

15

Daily Mail, 21 August 1917

Questions

1   Explain the terms Special Constable [**3.4, line 2**] and Defence of the Realm Act [**3.5, lines 1,2**].

2   What suggestion is made by the Chief Constable in Cardiff to deal with the worst effects of the dispute [**3.4**]? What arguments does he put forward to support it?

  (i) With reference to **3.6**, which of the newspapers is least hostile to the strikers? Give evidence to support your choice.

  (ii) What arguments against the strike are used by each newspaper? The *Daily Chronicle* and the *Daily Mail* both report, or guess at, hostile reactions from groups other than the strikers themselves. Which groups are these? Which do you think would be of most significance to the SLEF?

4   Which 'Laws of the Land' are specifically being broken by the strikers?

5   What light do the events recorded here shed on the efficacy of the Trade Union truce? Is it significant that this dispute is happening in a key and an effectively nationalised industry? (What records would be kept of troubles in small, or non-unionised industries? Would the Munitions Act have been invoked for any small industry?)

Conscientious Objectors

The issue which most transcended barriers of class, education and occupation is the subject of the third example of a divided society in this chapter. As we saw in Chapter 1, the questions of pacifism and compulsion were of major significance in the Liberal and Labour Parties. They also helped to divide the women's movement and the Christian denominations. Conscientious Objectors were neither a lunatic fringe nor a tiny clique, as the figures across show.

3.7 Conscientious Objectors before the Exemption Tribunal

Total population at 1911 census: approx 40,000,000
Total men in armed forces of UK: 6,100,000
Total number who went before Exemption Tribunals: 16,100

Outcome at the Exemption Tribunals (estimated)

200	absolute exemption
175	evasion of acts by changing identity, going into hiding, going abroad etc.
640	conditional exemption into Friends' Ambulance Unit (FAU) in France
740	exemption into other FAU groups
300	exemption into Royal Army Medical Corps or Quaker War Victims Relief Committee
3,300	exemption into Non-combatant Corps
3,964	exemption into Work of National Importance under Pelham Committee of Board of Trade
6,261	Absolutists, refusing to accept any verdict

Of the 6,261 Absolutists:

650	still in prison by May 1919
73	dead [10 *in prison*, 24 *in Home Office Centres*, 6 *in Military Custody*, 33 *shortly after release*]
20	certified insane by April 1919
11	in mental hospitals but not certified

Note These figures apply to the whole war. The numbers do not add up: some Conscientious Objectors abandoned their stance and went to war. The Absolutists were all in prison for the duration, and this table details the fate of only a few of them.

Based on Conscientious Objectors' Information Bureau figures

3.8

When a man has deliberately refused to avail himself of two alternative ways of escape from prison labour; when he has more than once, of his own deliberate choice, gone back to gaol; when he shows himself resolute to go back again and again rather than submit to that military service against which he asserts that his conscience raises for him an insuperable barrier – when he thus proves repeatedly his readiness to suffer for what he proclaims to be his beliefs, is it either justifiable or politic to go on with the punishment?

The Times, **25 October 1917**

Questions

1   With reference to **3.7,**
    (i) What proportion of the total Armed Forces number appeared before Tribunals?
    (ii) Do you think that the figure of 16,100 is an under- or over-estimate of people who had conscientious objections to the war? Give reasons for your conclusion.
    (iii) Approximately what proportion of the men who went before the Tribunals were Absolutists?
2   From your further reading, on what grounds might an applicant gain absolute exemption?
3   Discuss the reasons for harsh feelings against COs, and reasons why these feelings might have been changing, as in *The Times* article [3.8]. (The Imperial War Museum's Oral History archive has some fascinating tapes of memories by COs.)

Conscientious Objectors provoked stronger feelings than strikers; so too did the anti-conscription groups with which they were often associated. The Home Office was bombarded with requests to have anti-conscription meetings stopped under Section 9a of the Defence of the Realm Consolidation Regulations of 19 April 1916, which stated that:

3.9

Section 9a   Where there is reason to apprehend that the holding of a meeting in a public place will give rise to grave disorder and will thereby cause undue demands to be made upon the police or military forces, it shall be lawful for a Secretary of State, or for any Mayor, Magistrate or Chief Officer of Police who is duly authorised for the   5
purpose by a Secretary of State or for two or more such persons so authorised to make an order prohibiting the holding of the meeting and if a meeting is held or attempted to be held in contravention of any such prohibition, it shall be lawful to take such steps as may be necessary to disperse the meeting or prevent the holding thereof.   10

HO45/10810/311932/9

3.10   Advertisement for an anti-conscription meeting, 1916

A Demonstration will be made
in the Carfax, Horsham
(if wet in the Albion Hall)
on Friday June 9th 1916 at 8pm
in favour of the Repeal of the
Military Service Acts.

The Meeting will be addressed by

Miss E Sylvia Pankhurst
(East London Suffrage Federation),

Mr Alex Gossip
(Secretary of the Furnishing Trades' Union),

W. W. Kensett and others.

Horsham Council against Conscription.
W. W. Kensett, Secretary, 20 Bedford Road.

HO45/10810/311932/129245

Questions

1   What are the (very limited) circumstances in which a meeting can be stopped? What are the procedures necessary to stop a meeting [**3.9**]?
2   Look at the advertisement **3.10**.
   (i) Do you think this meeting would be likely to fall under the terms of Section 9a? (An application was in fact made by Horsham District Council to stop the meeting, but the request was rejected, having been annotated, in a laconic Home Office hand: 'I see no need for this –disturbance of the peace, and possibly of Miss S Pankhurst doesn't amount to grave disorder.')
   (ii) Why would the name Sylvia Pankhurst [**3.10**] have been likely to worry the authorities in Horsham?

But the meeting planned for the Cory Hall, Cardiff, on 11 November 1916 raised more interest. Study sources **3.11–3.15**, which tell the story of this meeting.

3.11   Circular advertising NCCL meeting

NATIONAL COUNCIL FOR CIVIL LIBERTIES

Dear Sir (or Madam),

A CONFERENCE will be held on Saturday, November 11th, at the Cory Hall, Cardiff, under the auspices of the above Council. To this Conference we are inviting delegates from Labour, Socialist, Co-operative and Religious Organisations.

The questions to be discussed will be under the following headings:−

1. **Industrial Conscription.**
2. **Maladministration of the Military Service Acts and their Repeal.**
3. **The Invasions of Personal and Civil Liberty.**
4. **Peace Negotiation.**

The National Council will be represented by the following:−

J. RAMSAY MACDONALD, M.P.
J. H. THOMAS, M.P.
Mrs H. M. SWANWICK, M.A.
Rev. Dr. WALTER WALSH
Rev. J. MORGAN JONES, M.A.

The Conference will be presided over by

MR. JAMES WINSTONE, J.P.,
President South Wales Miners' Federation

HO45/10810/311932

3.12   Part of a letter from Mr Williams, Head Constable, Cardiff City Police to the Home Office, 9 November 1916

The only feature which is likely to be provocative of disorder is the patriotic demonstration which will be held in Cathays Park simultaneously with the conference, and I am taking measures to prevent any clashing of the two parties.

Captain Atherley Jones is a patriot of an intense type and does not hesitate to hurl invective at anyone who he thinks is not patriotic, particularly the members of the National Council for Civil Liberties. His language at the demonstration on

5

Saturday may influence his audience to commit a breach of the peace,
but the police will be on the spot to deal with the matter.   10

I should add that I am informed that the National Council for
Civil Liberties was previously known as the National Council Against
Conscription, and it has been suggested that this change was made
because the original title was subject to misconstruction. On the other
hand, it might be said that the new title was adopted to beguile the   15
public.

HO45/10810/311932

3.13   Telegram received at the Home Office, 11 November 1916

As you have not seen fit to prohibit the pacifists' meeting to be
held at Cory Hall Cardiff today at two thirty, the seamen of this port
are taking the matter in their own hands and you must accept full
responsibility for what will certainly occur if meeting held, we refuse
to be held liable.   5
Edward Tupper, National Organiser, Seamen's Union and Matt
Terle, Cardiff Secretary.

HO45/10810/311932

3.14   Telegram received at the Home Office, 11 November 1916

As you have delegated your power under the Defence of the Realm
Act to the citizens of Cardiff they have smashed up the pro-German
conference at Cardiff today. Capt. Atherley Jones, Cardiff.

HO45/10810/311932/129245

The Times reported:

3.15

PATRIOTIC DEMONSTRATION
(FROM OUR SPECIAL CORRESPONDENT.)
CARDIFF, Nov. 11.

The people of Cardiff were fiercely indignant today at an attempt to
hold a conference in their city in favour of negotiations being
immediately begun to bring about an early peace. The conference hall
was stormed by an angry crowd and the meeting turned into a
patriotic demonstration.

The conference was organized by a body calling itself 'the National
Council for Civil Liberties'. It appears to be composed of representa-

tives of the Independent Labour Party, the Union of Democratic Control, the No-Conscription Fellowship, and the Fellowship of Reconciliation, and though, as its name implies, it purports to be concerned with the administration of the regulations made under the Defence of the Realm Act, its real object is to stop the war.

Among those who were to speak were Mr Ramsay MacDonald, M.P., Mr J. H Thomas, M.P., Mr J. E. Edmunds, and Mrs. H. M. Swanwick. But the conference speedily broke up in disorder, and instead of a resolution in support of an immediate peace one was carried declaring that the war must be prosecuted with the utmost vigour until the Germans were forced to accept the terms of the Allies unconditionally.

Of the 300 delegates expected not more than half put in an appearance. The conference was open to visitors on payment of 6d., and as soon as the speaking began, after the singing of the Socialist song, "Keep the Red Flag Flying," it was made clear that most of those who had paid to get in were hostile.

The real feelings of the people of Cardiff were expressed at a large meeting held on the open space at the City Hall. A declaration by Mr. STANTON, M.P., that it would be a lasting disgrace to Cardiff if a conference so repugnant to public opinion were allowed to be held, was endorsed by loud cheers and cries of "Down with the pro-German traitors!" and "We must be true to our boys in the trenches".

The Times, 13 November 1916

Questions

1   What topics were to be discussed at the conference [3.11]? Why would they be of concern to a range of people?

2   By referring to the article from *The Times* [3.15] and to the Circular [3.11] you can see how many organisations were invited to send delegates and how many in fact arrived. What does this tell you about the 'peace movement' and its support in the area?

3   What reasons are offered, both by *The Times* [3.15] and the Head Constable's letter [3.12] for the new name of the organisation? How do these two sources show their hostility to the NCCL?

4   Explain why the Head Constable did not feel it necessary to invoke Section 9a, and how he expected to avert or deal with any trouble [3.12].

5   The two telegrams [3.13 and 3.14] were sent at different times on the same day. How can you tell?

6   By using *The Times* article [3.15], show in detail how the telegrams were right and the police wrong about the meeting. What reasons for hostility were given by the crowds who broke up the meeting?

7   Discuss the value of considering a whole series of sources about one event, as has been possible in this chapter. Does it give a clearer picture? Or does it merely illuminate one corner, without clarifying the whole scene?

4 Propaganda and morale in the First World War

In the field of propaganda, as in social developments, the experience of the First World War was to be crucial to the decision makers of the Second. By 1919, there were few who doubted the effectiveness of British propaganda in the recent conflict. It was perceived to have been vital, not only in rallying civilian support for the war effort but also in undermining German morale both at the front and at home, and thus speeding up Germany's request for an armistice (for example, about two million leaflets had been dropped on Germany during 1917 and 1918).[1,2]

Given the importance later placed on propaganda by both sides, it is perhaps surprising that at the beginning of the war British efforts in the field of domestic propaganda were amateurish in the extreme. In 1914, the Central Committee for National Patriotic Organisations was set up, with the Prime Minister as Honorary President and Lord Rosebery and A. J. Balfour as Honorary Vice Presidents. It was not a government agency but its lectures and pamphlets were aimed at influencing public opinion, and were complemented by a massive outpouring of independent propaganda such as recruitment posters. This was produced spontaneously by the Press as well as other agencies, ranging from the Parliamentary Recruiting Committee and the London Electric Railway Company to Baroness Orczy's Society for Patriotic Girls.

Atrocity propaganda

The image of the martyred nurse, Edith Cavell, stretched lifeless at the feet of a brutal German Officer with a smoking pistol in his hand, was popularised by postcards and newspaper headlines. Indeed, the death of the renowned cricketer W. G. Grace on 23 October 1915 was virtually pushed off the front pages by the Cavell story. The basic inaccuracies of the story were ignored. Edith Cavell was in fact tied to a firing post, blindfolded, and shot by four bullets from a firing squad, six paces away. She had been found guilty by a German military court of abusing her position as a nurse in Belgium, in order to assist Allied soldiers to escape from the German occupying forces.

Accounts of brutality against the general population, particularly women and children, were staples of early atrocity propaganda.

4.1

4.2

At Tirlemont another Englishman ... met a peasant woman who told him that her babes had been trampled to death under the hoofs of the horses of Uhlans. As the Englishman was considering that he had only the woman's word for this atrocity, he saw a little girl come staggering along the road as if she were blind. He found her eye and cheek were laid open. This had been done, not by a chance bullet, but by a deliberate thrust of an Uhlan's lance, who charged upon the innocent child in sheer devilish sport.

The War Illustrated, Vol 1, no. 3, 5 September 1914

Questions

1   (i) What specific accusations are being made in **4.1** against the Germans?
    (ii) When had these alleged atrocities taken place?
2   By what means does poster **4.1** attempt to convince readers that these stories are true?
3   Identify the emotive words used in **4.2**. What more neutral words could have been used?
4   How convincing do you think contemporary readers would have found material like **4.1** and **4.2**? Do you think they would have influenced civilian behaviour in any significant way? Explain your conclusion.

Official propaganda and the Ministry of Information

As early as 14 August 1914, the Cabinet had decided to initiate official propaganda. The Liberal politician C. F. G. Masterman was appointed head of propaganda and his office, working from the National Health Insurance Commission in Wellington House, began to produce material for domestic as well as foreign consumption. A serious attempt was made to discover the truth behind the atrocity stories, but with little success. Not until the 1920s were most of these stories revealed as the lies they were. The news department of the Foreign Office was also involved in propaganda, mainly for foreign consumption. War correspondents were taken to the front in May 1915, and 'official' photographs began to be issued, in contrast to the earlier War Office and Admiralty ban on all photographers. By the Autumn of 1916, 4,000 official photographs were being issued weekly, and there were six weekly illustrated newspapers [**4.2**], selling between them one million copies.

The agencies overseeing the production of propaganda worked with little government interference until 1916, when enthusiasm for the war was seen to be flagging. Lloyd George then created a Department of Information to supervise the various agencies concerned with raising morale, controlling news and producing films. Soon afterwards, the National War Aims Committee was established, which took over the functions of the Central Committee for National Patriotic Organisations. Even this was not enough for Lloyd George, far more interested in propaganda than Churchill would ever be, and in April 1918 he set up the Ministry of Information under Lord Beaverbrook.

Beaverbrook developed the myth that he had 'invented' propaganda.

4.3

> There was no blueprint to work on; no experience to guide the new department. There was no office, no staff. There was nothing but a decision of the War Cabinet that such a Ministry should be created, and that I should be the Minister.
>
> **Lord Beaverbrook, *Men and Power*, 1956**

In point of fact, by the time the Ministry was established, there was considerable experience and expertise for it to draw on, and much thought had been given to its functions.

An anonymous memorandum in the House of Lords Record Office of March/July 1918 reads:

4.4

> The function of propaganda is the formation of public opinion. The method is to tell the truth, but to present it in an acceptable form. It is useless to imagine that the mere existence of a fact will penetrate everywhere by its own weight, or that facts themselves do not require treatment according to the audience to which they are to be presented.
>
> **HLRO/BBKE-11/300, quoted in Nicholas Reeves, *Official British Film Propaganda during World War 1*, 1986**

5

Questions

1   Summarise, from this chapter, and from your other reading, the various areas of 'experience' on which Beaverbrook could in fact draw.

2   Why would Beaverbrook [4.3] present his experience in this light in his memoirs?

3 Comment on the accuracy of the definition of propaganda in **4.4**. In what ways have the various examples of propaganda with which you are familiar been 'treated' according to their probable audience?

The role of cinema

The newest medium for informing and influencing the masses, as the war began, was the cinema. Students who wish to enlarge upon the brief summary in this chapter are recommended to refer to Nicholas Reeves' masterly study, *Official British Film Propaganda during World War 1*,[3] which gives a much more complete picture than there is room for here.

By 1917 there were 4,500 'theatres' in Britain (compared to 21,000 in the USA and 1,000 in Russia): each member of the public could – in theory – visit a cinema once in every fourteen days, although not all the population was in fact within reach of a cinema. It took some time for British propaganda agencies to appreciate the value of the medium, in spite of the fact that commercial companies rapidly realised that adventure and romance films were easily made by converting the dastardly villains into Prussians and the gallant heroines into Belgians, or VADs (Voluntary Aid Detachments). As early as 14 April 1915 an article in *The Times* recommended the use of film, referring to the impact of German films on audiences in neutral countries. It was not, however, until 29 December 1915 that the film *Britain Prepared* was premiered, before an invited audience at the Empire Music Hall in Leicester Square, London, with the first Lord of the Admiralty making a speech in the interval. After this auspicious start, *Britain Prepared* showed to full audiences every afternoon until 12 February, and was then booked by 100 cinemas, on a strictly commercial basis.

The most striking film of the war, however, was almost certainly the *Battle of the Somme*, because it was the first actually to show trench warfare, the explosion of mines, the wounded and even the dead.

Among the first people to see the film, on 2 August 1916, was Frances Stevenson, Lloyd George's secretary (and mistress). She wrote in her diary:

4.5

August 4, 1916
We went on Wednesday night to a private view of the Somme films, i.e. the pictures taken during recent fighting. To say that one enjoyed them would be untrue; but I am glad I went. I am glad I have seen the sort of thing our men have to go through, even to the sortie from the trench and the falling in the barbed wire. There were pictures too 5

of the battlefield after the fight and of our gallant men lying crumpled and helpless. There were pictures of men mortally wounded being carried out of the communication trenches with the look of agony on their faces. It reminded me of what Paul's [her brother] last hours were. I have often tried to imagine to myself what he went through, but now I know: and I shall never forget. It was like going through a tragedy. I felt something of what the Greeks must have felt when they went in their crowds to witness those grand old plays – to be purged in their minds through pity and terror. 10

A. J. P. Taylor (ed.), *Lloyd George: A Diary by Frances Stevenson,* **1971**

Here are some of the captions from the film, not as a substitute for seeing the film, but to give the flavour of it:

4.6   Captions 8–10, 14, 31–6 to *Battle of the Somme*, 1916

Caption 8 Along the entire front the munition 'dumps' are receiving vast supplies of shells, thanks to British munition workers.

Caption 9 Hidden batteries were pounding the German trenches for five days before the attack of 1 July. Re-filling limbers with 18 pounder shells, after 'dumping' the empty cases.

Caption 10 A divisional General addressing the Lancashire Fusiliers and Royal Fusiliers. A Battalion of the Hampshires moving up to the attack.

Caption 14 Meanwhile, more troops are started for the trenches. London Scottish and East Yorkshires. Manchester's Church Service evening before the attack.

Caption 31 A sunken road in 'no man's land' occupied by the Lancashire Fusiliers. (20 minutes after this picture was taken, these men came under heavy machine gun fire.)

Caption 32 Warwickshires advancing up a captured trench to relieve the Queens in the front line.

Caption 33 The attack. At a signal, along the entire sixteen-mile front, the troops leaped over the trench parapets and advanced towards the German trenches, under heavy fire of the enemy.

Caption 34 British Tommies rescuing a comrade under shell fire. (This man died 30 minutes after reaching the trenches.) Conveying wounded by wheeled stretchers.

Caption 35 Bringing in the wounded (British and Germans) on stretchers through the trenches during the height of battle. German wounded being brought in near Carnoy.

Caption 36 A Lancashire Battalion which has been relieved after a successful attack, returns with prisoners. Friend and foe help each other.

The film was screened simultaneously in thirty London cinemas, and by October had 2,000 bookings all over the country, again seen as a commercial proposition by the hiring cinemas. Suggestions in the Press that it was gory and gruesome were refuted by the public response, with letters to the newspapers along the lines of Frances Stevenson's diary entry. The later film, *Battle of the Ancre*, was screened in 112 London cinemas at once.

By April 1918, ten lorries (later twenty) had been equipped to make cine motor tours. A twenty-five foot screen would be erected one hundred feet from the projector/generator lorry, and official films were shown to average audiences of 3,000: probably as many as 163,000 people per week saw these films. Many viewers brought their own imaginations to play upon what they saw, like this schoolboy, who described the film of the Battle of the Ancre:

4.7 Battle of the Ancre

Now the whistle shrills and they leap over the parapet; rat, tap, tap go the machine guns, but nothing daunts our soldiers. Crack! and their gallant Captain falls. This enrages the men to fury. At last they reach the German lines. Most of the Germans flee for their lives shouting Kamerad, Kamerad! etc. Now the British and German wounded are brought in, some seriously, some slightly. Soon after follow German prisoners, some vicious looking scoundrels that I should not like to meet on a dark night, others, young boys about 16 years of age.

Quoted in *The Cinema: its present position and future possibilities*, being the report and chief evidence of an enquiry instituted by the National Council of Public Morals.

(Nicholas Reeves, who quotes the above, adds: 'Looking at the film now, it is impossible to recognise it in this account; drawing on the whole series of other images of war, the boy has welded them together to develop an account of a film which existed only in his own imagination.'[3])

Questions

1   Compare the responses to the films of **4.5** and **4.7**. What evidence of the background and education of each writer can you extract from what they say?

2   What do you think was the motive underlying the following points about the captions, and the sequences of film they describe [**4.6**]?
      (i) Naming specific regiments.
      (ii) The various references to shells and munitions.
      (iii) Mention of what happens after the filming of shots shown.
      (iv) Reference to German and British troops helping each other.

3   Discuss the type of audience likely to be reached by film as opposed to other forms of information.

4   What purpose might be served by showing 'the people' some of the 'horrors of war'? Do you think this aspect of propaganda is affected by the fact of conscription from the beginning of 1916 onwards? Justify your answer.

This chapter has offered for consideration only a fraction of the types of propaganda put before the British people. More examples of official and unofficial information can be found in the sections about women, industry and recruiting. Despite its limitations, this chapter should enable the reader to think about the different targets and aims of propaganda, and to begin to consider, however impressionistically, the likely impact of propaganda on a population which was experiencing mass warfare and conscription for the first time in its history, and which had benefited from compulsory schooling since 1881 at the latest.

Summary exercise

Make a table to summarise all the sources from which civilians could extract information about the war. It should evaluate the probable accuracy and limitations of each source, identify its target groups, and consider its likely impact, both in terms of numbers likely to see it, and innate effectiveness.

References

1   Field Marshal P. von Hindenburg, *Out of My Life*, Cassell, 1920
2   Sir Campbell Stuart, *Secrets of Crewe House*, Hodder and Stoughton, London, 1920
3   N. Reeves, *Official British Film Propaganda during World War I*, Croom Helm and Imperial War Museum, 1986

5 Government and politics in the Second World War

The effect the Second World War had on British government and politics appears obvious. Consider the facts: in September 1939 Chamberlain's predominantly Conservative National government had 418 seats in the House of Commons; Labour had 167. In the 1945 General Election, Labour won 393 seats, the Conservatives only 213. The Conservative Winston Churchill had formed a Coalition of all Parties in May 1940, which appeared to work harmoniously together under his dynamic leadership. Yet a study of the period raises many difficult questions. Did Labour come into politics in 1940 as an inferior group who used the experience of war to hijack power? Or did they, as Paul Addison suggests, enter into a partnership as nearly equals so that, as early as 1940, the foundation of political power shifted decisively leftward for a decade and the Conservatives lost all hope of post-war control by 1942?[1] How did the machinery of government adapt itself to wartime necessities and exigencies? What effect did the war have on the main political parties and how well did they co-operate at all levels?

This chapter attempts to present readers with a variety of evidence which will help them to understand just how difficult it is for any student of the period to be dogmatic on the above issues. Readers will be provided with illustrations of the ways in which usual kinds of party conflict gave way to co-operation. At the same time it will be seen that not all political tensions were lost in wartime. Chamberlain's government from 1937 to his fall in 1940 has been considered by Paul Adelman in a companion volume[2] and it is not proposed to duplicate that work here. Suffice it to say that, by the time he fell from power, Chamberlain had lost the confidence of the Opposition and many of his own party (on 8 May 1940 his majority in the Commons fell from over 200 to 81). The next few weeks saw the defeat of the British army and, by 4 June, its evacuation from the beaches of Dunkirk.

It is important to remember that this was the position Churchill inherited in 1940 and it was his personality which dominated all aspects of war until his electoral defeat in May 1945. Without an understanding of the role played by this one man, his public leadership, the control he exercised over his Coalition Cabinet and his command of strategy, it is impossible to understand the nature of wartime domestic politics. This chapter concentrates, therefore, on Churchill as war leader. Students interested in the 1945 General Election and the role of the Labour Party leader, Clement Attlee, should consult Paul Adelman.[2]

Churchill as war leader

When Churchill became Prime Minister on 10 May 1940 few of his Conservative colleagues had the foresight to welcome him on his entrance to the Commons; many were outspoken in their preference for Halifax (Foreign Secretary, 1938–40). Within a few weeks, however, he had established so strong a hold over the hearts and minds of the public, that he became a legend, one that has endured to the present day, despite attempts to portray him as a drunken war-monger.[3] He dominated politics, strategy and diplomacy to such an extent contemporaries and some later historians have found it difficult to assess his role without uncritical adulation [5.1, 5.2] and there has always been the temptation, avoided in 5.3, of attributing to one man the achievements of a whole nation. Consider the following assessments of his role:

5.1

> I think it is fitting that today I should pay tribute to one of the main
> architects of our victory. However we may be divided politically in
> this House, I believe I shall be expressing the views of the whole
> House in making acknowledgement here of the transcendent services
> rendered by the Right Hon. gentleman to this country, to the Com-   5
> monwealth and Empire, and to the world during his tenure of office.
>   During those years he was leader of the country in war. We have
> seen in Fascist countries a detestable cult of leadership which has
> only been a cover for dictatorship, but there is a true leadership
> which means the expression by one man of the soul of a nation, and   10
> its translation of the common will into action. In the darkest and
> most dangerous hours of our history this nation found in my Right
> Hon. friend the man who expressed supremely the courage and
> determination never to yield which animated all the men and the
> women of this country. In undying phrases he crystallised the   15
> unspoken feeling of all. 'Words only,' it might be said, but words of
> great moment in history are deeds. We had more than words from
> the Right Hon. gentleman. He radiated a stream of energy through-
> out the machinery of government, indeed throughout the life of the
> nation.   20

Many others shared in the work of organising and inspiring the nation in its great effort, but he set the pace. He was able to bring into co-operation men of very different political views and to win from them loyal service. At critical times, by his personal relationship with the heads of allied States, he promoted the harmony and co-operation of all, and in the sphere of strategy his wide experience, grasp of essentials, his willingness to take necessary risks were of the utmost value ... His place in history is secure.

C. R. Attlee speaking in the House of Commons, 16 August 1945,
***Hansard*, 5th series, Vol 413, cols 96–7**

25

5.2

While western Europe collapsed under the weight of Hitler's assault, Britain alone, against the expectations of the entire world, resisted the advance of Nazism. In that achievement Churchill's own part was inestimable. He alone, by example and exhortation, transformed a demoralised nation into one of inflexible resolution.

5

David Mason, *Churchill*, 1973, editorial comment on the back cover of the book

5.3

In that dark time of disaster, Winston Churchill shone by his fighting spirit. But although full recognition should be given to the example he set, it would be a mistake to equate this, in a historical judgement of events, with its influence on the situation. The British have always been less dependent than other people upon inspiring leadership. Their record embraces relatively few spectacular victories but they have a unique record of winning 'soldiers' battles'. The fact of being 'up against it' with their backs to the wall has repeatedly proved sufficient to rally them. Thus, in their case, inspiring leadership may be regarded as an additional asset rather than a necessity. It may be a necessity when they are weary, but not when they have had a slap in the face. It was Dunkirk that braced them in June 1940, more than any individual influence.

5

10

Basil Liddell Hart, in A. J. P. Taylor *et al.*, *Churchill, Four Faces and the Man*, 1969

Questions

1   List the main roles Attlee ascribes to Churchill as a war leader [5.1].
2   On what do the assessments of Churchill's role agree [5.1 and 5.2]?
3   From extract **5.1**,
   (i) How well did Churchill work with 'men of very different political views' [**line 23**]?
   (ii) How important was his 'personal relationship with the heads of allied States' [**lines 24–25**] in his role as leader of Britain in wartime?
4   Compare the tone of the three documents [5.1–5.3] and identify the main differences between their estimation of Churchill's achievements.
5   How do the following facts affect your views of the usefulness of Attlee's assessment of Churchill's role as war leader?
   (i) Attlee was the only man apart from Churchill himself who sat in Churchill's wartime Cabinet from first to last.
   (ii) Attlee was the leader of the Labour Party and politically opposed to Churchill.
   (iii) During the war Attlee observed a political truce.
   (iv) Attlee often deputised for Churchill when he was absent, taking the chair at the War Cabinet and acting as leader of the Commons.
6   From your wider reading, consider how Attlee's and Churchill's positions had changed by August 1945. Do you think this would affect
   (i) Attlee's public statements about Churchill such as 5.1?
   (ii) the usefulness of Attlee's views to historians attempting to obtain an objective view of Churchill?
7   These sources [5.1–5.3] are produced for three different types of purposes. Assess the usefulness of each one to a student attempting to reach some kind of understanding of Churchill's role in wartime Britain.

Churchill's popularity remained extraordinarily high even when the country suffered military defeats, increased rationing and bombing [5.4]. His image became synonymous with patriotism [5.5].

5.4 Gallup Poll, 1941

84 Per Cent
Still Approve Churchill
As Premier

How little Mr. Winston Churchill's personal prestige as Prime Minister has suffered with the public as a result of the recent criticism of the Government is shown by a Gallup Poll. The usual question was asked:

"In general, do you approve or disapprove of Mr. Churchill as Prime Minister?"

The British Institute of Public Opinion, which takes the Gallup Poll in this country, found that of the total questioned:

84 p.c. said   "Approve"

11 p.c. said   "Disapprove"

5 p.c. said   "Don't know"

Before this, the most recent poll on this question was taken in June, 1941. The results then were: Approve, 87 per cent.: Disapprove, 9 per cent.: Don't know, 4 per cent.

★

How consistently high Mr. Churchill has stood in the country throughout the past year of office as Prime Minister is shown by the tabulation of six Polls,

taken at varying intervals during the 12 months, given below:

	Approve	Disap-prove	Don't know
Oct., 1940 ...	89	6	5
Nov., 1940 ...	88	7	5
Feb., 1941 ...	85	7	8
March, 1941	88	7	5
June, 1941 ...	87	9	4
Oct., 1941 ...	84	11	5

The maintenance of such high public confidence in Mr. Churchill as Premier is in marked contrast with the recent sharp decline in public satisfaction with the conduct of the war by the Government as a whole.

★

In a Gallup Poll published in the News Chronicle on October 23 it was revealed that the percentage professing themselves satisfied with the Government's conduct of the war was only 44 per cent., with 28 per cent. dissatisfied, and 18 per cent. giving no opinion.

This shows a drop of 14 per cent. in those satisfied as compared with the previous Poll taken in June, 1941, when 58 per cent. said they were satisfied with the Government's conduct of the war.

In the same Poll, published on October 23, only 29 per cent. of those questioned said they thought that Britain had taken full advantage of the opportunities offered by the German attack on Russia.

British Institute of Public Opinion.

News Chronicle, **3 November 1941**

5.5   Poster issued by London Transport, 1943

OUR HERITAGE

We shall go on to the end, **we shall fight in France, we shall fight on the seas and oceans, we shall fight with growing confidence and growing strength in the air,** we shall defend our island, whatever the cost may be, **we shall fight on the beaches, we shall fight on the landing grounds, we shall fight in the fields and in the streets, we shall fight in the hills;** we shall never surrender . . . until, in God's good time, the new world, with all its power and might, steps forth to the rescue and the liberation of the old.

The Rt. Hon. WINSTON S. CHURCHILL, P.C., M.P., after the collapse of France, June, 1940

Questions

1   With reference to **5.4**:
    (i) by how much had public satisfaction with the government dropped between June and October 1941?
    (ii) how far had Churchill's popularity declined in the same period?
    (iii) how do you account for (a) the difference between Churchill's popularity and that of his government, (b) the fact that the former did not apparently decline as much as the latter?
    (iv) what factors could account for the drop in popularity of both in this period?
2   Given the fact that a Gallup Poll is a sample of the population,
    (i) how accurate do you think it would have been in 1941?
    (ii) how useful are such opinion polls generally to the historian?
3   Look at **5.5**.
    (i) Make a list of the methods used in the poster to give an impression of Churchill as a leader and statesman.
    (ii) Why do you think London Transport issued such a poster?
4   Compare the way the newspaper [**5.4**] and the poster [**5.5**] present an impression of Churchill. Do you consider this type of evidence to be of any use to a historian
    (i) investigating the reasons for the success of Churchill as a war leader?
    (ii) attempting to discover what people thought of Churchill in wartime?
5   'Both the newspaper and poster are propaganda. This invalidates their usefulness to a historian.' Discuss.

Attempts to account for Churchill's political and popular supremacy are often too facile. Take, for example, the assumption so often made, that Churchill's position depended a great deal on his mastery of language. There is little doubt that his speeches inspired the British people. Yet he himself, though taking great pains with his delivery of them to the House of Commons, appeared indifferent to their impact on the public. Asa Briggs has pointed out that, in his six volumes of *The Second World War*, Churchill referred only nine times to the role of broadcasting and never to his own broadcasts.[4] He just did not think they were important. Many of his most famous speeches, for example the one delivered to the Commons on 4 June 1940 which contained the immortal lines 'we shall fight on the beaches, we shall fight on the landing grounds

... we shall never surrender ...' [5.5] were aimed primarily at fellow MPs and were only broadcast later to the public.

Although his words were repeated in the Press [8.8] and quoted freely by those who read them, their immediate impact was on the House of Commons where they helped to establish his leadership.

The reasons for Churchill's unique position in the period 1940–45 are many. He was a skilled politician who presided over a disparate Cabinet, a statesman who established good working relationships with Roosevelt and Stalin, and above all he was a war leader who planned strategy – A. J. P. Taylor includes him among the 'warlords'[5]. Evidence suggests, however, that not unsurprisingly he was unable to exercise all these roles effectively [5.6, 5.7]. Some even question whether his personality, charismatic though it was, was of key importance [5.3].

By accepting the leadership of the Conservative Party in October 1940, Churchill assured his power base in the House of Commons. Was he 'a blood transfusion for an exhausted and demoralised Party',[1] or did he effectively castrate it by refusing to be interested in reconstruction and allowing Labour Ministers to spearhead planning for the post-war world? How did Labour leaders manage to persuade their rank and file to continue to support a government so patently uninterested in Beveridge and other social reform? Conversely how did the Cabinet soothe back-bench Tory anxieties that the Labour leaders were using the Trojan horse of the Coalition to establish socialism in the name of expediency? Many of the tensions were, no doubt, suppressed by immediate wartime dangers and the struggle of the nation to survive. Yet they remained to surface when the pressure of war lessened.

The Labour Party did well out of the war and Addison goes so far as to say that the war 'saw a reformation of English politics for a generation',[1] bringing about as it did a leftward shift of public opinion and a victory for Labour in 1945. For Churchill the Home Front was peripheral to his one aim – victory. He gladly handed over responsibility for domestic issues to his Ministers [5.6, 5.7], some of the most important of whom were Labour, occasionally interfering when things went wrong. His most inspired appointment was Bevin (General Secretary of the TGWU) as Minister of Labour. Morrison (Leader of the London County Council 1934–40) as Home Secretary was another success, and Attlee, gaining valuable administrative experience and political credibility as Deputy Prime Minister, emerged from the war as a respected, if unspectacular states-man, a perfect foil to Churchill's ebullient style of leadership. Many of the successful measures adopted as necessary in wartime, such as rationing, appeared not only fair but desirable to the populace and helped accustom them to socialist principles. Yet the Labour Party itself was often divided.

Morrison and Bevin hated one another, and there grew up among the backbench Labour MPs a distrust of the way their Ministers appeared to acquiesce too readily to Churchill's demands that reconstruction questions be postponed until after the war, manifesting itself in a rebellion in February 1943 of the Parliamentary Labour Party against the government's lukewarm treatment of the Beveridge report.

Even when his government presided over some of the worst defeats the British have faced, Churchill was rarely challenged. Partly the strength of his position lay in the fact that there was no-one else of his stature to take over. 'God knows where we should be without him,' his CIGS (Chief of Imperial General Staff)-designate, Alanbrooke, wrote on 4 December 1941, though he added 'God knows where we shall go with him'.[6] Supreme as leader of his party, Churchill enjoyed the support of a loyal group of Labour and Liberal Cabinet colleagues who, as late as December 1944, hoped that the Coalition would continue at least until the defeat of Japan, if not longer. Nevertheless there were considerable strains within such a government and there are several interesting issues raised by the nature of Churchill's leadership. How did he unite such a diverse group of politicians? What effect did his leadership have on the Conservative and Labour parties?

To the public Churchill was usually presented as an efficient and effective leader. There is evidence, however, that he, not surprisingly, found it difficult to be as competent in running his government as the public believed him to be. Consider the extract below from the diary of Robert Menzies, the Australian Prime Minister (1939–41). On a visit to Britain, Menzies occasionally attended the War Cabinet and thus had first-hand knowledge of Churchill's methods of government.

5.6   Diary of Robert Menzies, 26 April 1941

Drove down to Churt to lunch with Lloyd George, who is as clear headed as ever, and has some shrewd things to say about Cabinet organisation, Winston's leadership, and the like. We found we had many ideas in common, much as follows:

1   Winston is acting as the master strategist, without qualification   5
and without really forceful Chiefs of Staff to guide him.

2   Dill [Sir John Dill, Chief of the Imperial General Staff] has
ability, but is as timid as a hare.

3   There is no War Cabinet, since WC deals with conduct of war
himself, by 'directives' etc., and his Ministers just concur.   10

4   Beaverbrook might have some influence but he is up to the neck
in the detail of aircraft construction, and simply has no time for
general study and appreciation. No War Cabinet Minister here
should have anything to attend to except War Cabinet.

5   War Cabinet should meet every morning. This week, this crucial   15
and anxious week it has met twice for an hour and $1\frac{1}{2}$ hours
respectively!

6   Winston should be at the helm, instead of touring the bombed
areas, as he has been doing most of the week. Let the King and
Queen do this. In any case they do it much better.   20

7   More food could be grown in this country, but there is nobody
finally responsible for comprehensive policy, which must include
food, agriculture, fisheries and so on. Many ministers, many opinions.
Same with shipping. M/Shipping attends to the fag end – eg charter
parties – Admiralty builds and mends ships, Labour controls labour,   25
Transport the getting of goods off the wharves, Supply what can be
carried on the ships etc. etc. In brief, Churchill is a bad organiser.

8   A non-executive War Cabinet *must* contain a Dominions man,
for the Dominions type of mind is essential.

9   The problem of a couple of good men to prop up Churchill is   30
acute. He is not interested in finance, economics, agriculture, and
ignores the debates on all three. He loves war and spends hours with
the maps and charts, working out fresh combinations. He has aggression without knowledge or at any rate without any love for inconve-
nient knowledge. His advisers are presumed to have knowledge, but   35
haven't enough aggression to convey it to Churchill.

10   Foreign policy is deplorable – eg Japan. We never have ideas,
and we never beat Germany to it. Alex Cadogan [Permanent Under
Secretary at the Foreign Office] is a dull dog, if not actually a dead
dog.   40

11   Eden [Foreign Secretary] has not (?trained) on [diary unclear],
and John Anderson [Lord President of the Council, formerly Home
Secretary] is a bureaucrat par excellence – no imagination, or sweep,
or fire.

Quoted in David Day, *Menzies and Churchill at War*, 1986

Menzies and Lloyd George were neither in the government nor intimates
of Churchill however, and maybe their judgements, although apparently
in accord, need to be viewed with caution. Hugh Dalton, part of whose
diary is reproduced in 5.7, was a Labour Minister in Churchill's government (first as Minister for Economic Warfare and then at the Board of
Trade). He attended Cabinet meetings regularly.

5.7 Diary of Hugh Dalton, 19 May 1944

War Cabinet at noon. The Full Employment White Paper, called
'Employment Policy', is finally – repeat finally – approved, subject to
Woolton and Anderson putting in some extra sentence to meet the
Beaver's view that not quite enough is said about the need to stimulate private investment if trade looks like drooping. The PM admits   5
that [he] has not read the paper and that he asked the Prof for a short
note on it, but that the Prof has produced a very long note, and that
he has not had time to read this either. But he has read the first
sentence, in which the Prof says that he regards this as a very bold
and ably conceived plan worthy of full support. The PM adds that he   10
notices that the Committee which prepared this plan 'contained all
the best brain power in the Cabinet', but, before finally committing
himself, he would like to hear the view of the Lord Privy Seal, who
was not on the Committee. The latter says that he regards this as 'a
magnificent scheme, a first-class scheme', and we should all certainly   15
support it. Woolton [Minister of Reconstruction: no political al-
legiance] then begins to give some general explanations, dwelling in
particular on the proposed variation in the social service contributions
according to the state of trade. The PM says he understands that
what is proposed for public authorities is the exact opposite of what   20
would be generally done by private persons, that when things look
bad, they should not draw in their horns but push them out and
launch forth into all sorts of new expenditures. Woolton replies that
this is exactly so, and that it will be necessary to do a good deal of
education of the public mind upon it. The PM says 'I suppose that at   25
such times it would be helpful to have a series of Cabinet banquets –
a sort of Salute the Stomach Week?' Amid the laughter following this
happy quip, the White Paper is approved for publication.

Ben Pimlott (ed.), *The Second World War Diaries of Hugh Dalton,*
1940–45, 1986

Questions

1 With reference to **5.6**:
  (i) identify the main criticisms made of Churchill
  (ii) to what extent are Menzies' criticisms based on first-hand
     evidence, to what extent on rumour and prejudice?
2 Why, and with what justification, did Menzies believe British foreign
  policy towards Japan was deplorable [**5.6**]?

3   Comment on the tone of Menzies' diary [5.6].
4   From **5.6** and your own reading, consider Beaverbrook's influence in Churchill's government and his relationship with the Prime Minister during the war years.
5   In extract **5.7**, who was
     (i) the Prof?
     (ii) the Privy Seal?
     (iii) Woolton?
     (iv) Anderson?
6   What light does **5.7** cast on
     (i) Churchill's priorities?
     (ii) the way decisions were made in Cabinet?
     (iii) Churchill's relationship with his Ministers?
7   To what extent were criticisms of Churchill's leadership in **5.6** supported by Dalton's comments in **5.7**?
8   Consider the usefulness or otherwise to historians of diaries in general as historical evidence.

Tensions in the Coalition

For most of the war Churchill, aided loyally by Attlee and Labour, and supported by the Liberals, led a united Coalition. Yet there were tensions which surfaced occasionally in Commons' debates and, more often, in Cabinet between the main parties. Nor were these always the result of Labour disquiet with Churchill's Tory leadership. On 21 April 1941, Hugh Dalton, President of the Board of Trade, fearing lest coal stocks run out the following winter, promoted a scheme by Beveridge for coal rationing. The plan received Cabinet approval but he was shocked at the way in which Conservative back-benchers denounced it. The following are all extracts from his diary. (Note that at the end of the diary extracts, on page 78, there are details of the main characters whom Dalton mentions.)

5.8(a)   Wednesday 6 May 1941

A word with Butler who says that the Tories are against fuel rationing because they are afraid that it will mean that they won't get enough for their country houses. If I could offer them not only the proposed household ration but also some based on a datum period, they would all agree. I repeat this to Gaitskell who thinks it absolutely true and most disgraceful. If I were to quote it outside, he says, it would do great damage.

5

Early this morning I tabulate a list of reasons for the resistance among the Tories, to the Beveridge Plan. [NB Coal rationing, not the social insurance proposals outlined in the later Beveridge Report of 1942.]   10

1   An instinctive feeling against the rationing of coal.
2   A dislike of miners; why can't they work harder?
3   A dislike of coupons and 'officials'.
4   A dislike of Labour Ministers in general (the *Daily Telegraph* is   15
now daily gunning against one or other of us, Morrison, or me, or in this same group, Cripps; one of the methods is a selective printing of hostile letters).
5   Some dislike of me in particular, though with many Tory MPs I am the most popular of the Labour Ministers, but a recognition that   20
I am rather 'clever' and a fear that I am trying to put through nationalisation of the mines by a side wind. (The Labour Party, on the other hand, think that rationing may be a device for evading nationalisation by a side wind) . . .

Ben Pimlott (ed.), *The Second World War Diaries of Hugh Dalton,*
1940–45, **1986**

Dalton felt too isolated to continue the fight for rationing alone and he conceived of an idea to postpone the plan until he could place before the House a complete programme covering production, consumption and organisation. He sought allies for this idea:

5.8(b)   Tuesday 12 May

I . . . proceed to the House to answer my questions at 11, the Cabinet being at noon. I canvas both Attlee and Cripps on the Bench, and get their agreement. Likewise Kingsley Wood, emerging from the lavatory, in a walk down the passage. Likewise Anderson, with whom I have a longer talk in his room. He has a new coal fear. There may   5
soon be large numbers of American soldiers in this country desirous of heating themselves up to the temperature they are accustomed to in the USA. He says that it is being said by Tories that I only got the support of the Labour Party to rationing by telling them that the alternative was a lengthening of miners' hours, which otherwise the   10
Tories would propose. I tell him that this is quite untrue. (Another rumour running about these days is that I got the Labour Party to support rationing because I told them nationalisation would soon follow!) . . .

At the Cabinet we spend an hour and twenty minutes on this one 15
subject. I have never thought so ill of the PM, nor been so vexed by
him before. He talks more than half the time, and has clearly not
concentrated his mind on the details of the subject at all ... He
argues at immense length, almost alone, against a substantial majority
of his colleagues. He is quite unconvinced of the need of any ration- 20
ing. He thinks that a broadcast appeal by himself would do the trick,
followed up by a press campaign. We explain at tedious length that at
this season of the year it is important to stock up and that it is
impossible to be sure whether coal goes into the cellars, as it should,
or the grate, as it should not. Therefore it would not be possible for 25
months to determine whether his appeal had succeeded or not. And
then it would be too late. To this he can only reply that the Air Raid
Wardens could carry out inspections of people's cellars to see whether
they were storing or burning coal. He has received a letter from
Dugdale, Chairman of the Tory Party organisation, saying that the 30
feelings of the Party are very strong against the Beveridge scheme ...
The PM says that last year they were told that things would be very
awkward in the winter, and yet they weren't. Why should it be any
worse this time?

Eden is very wobbly, and Lyttleton significantly silent during this 35
discussion. Anderson, Bevin, Cripps and I, with faint support from
Attlee, put the other view. Sinclair, called in to represent the Liberal
Party is also more or less on our side. I, however, present the view, at
an early stage of the meeting, that we should postpone the decision ... This is rather gratefully accepted by most ... 40

Ben Pimlott (ed.), ***The Second World War Diaries of Hugh Dalton,***
1940–45, **1986**

Characters mentioned in Dalton's diary, in alphabetical order, and the positions
they held in May 1941.

Sir John Anderson, Lord President, Conservative
Clement Attlee, Leader of the Labour Party and, in effect, deputy Prime Minister
Ernest Bevin, Minister of Labour and National Service, Labour
R. A. Butler, Parliamentary Under Secretary in the Foreign Office, Conservative
Stafford Cripps, Ambassador to Moscow, Labour
Sir Anthony Eden, Secretary of State for Foreign Affairs, Conservative
Hugh Gaitskill, Principal Private Secretary to the Minister of Economic Warfare,
    Labour
Oliver Lyttleton, President of the Board of Trade, Conservative
Herbert Morrison, Secretary of State for the Home Office, Labour
Sir Archibald Sinclair, Secretary of State for Air, Liberal
Sir Kingsley Wood, Chancellor of the Exchequer, Conservative

In the end compromise was reached. A White Paper on coal giving the government more control over mining operations left the finances with the mine owners and rationing was never introduced. This incident was the only successful Conservative revolt against the Churchill administration. The Coalition survived intact.

On 7 October 1944 the Labour Party National Executive Committee stated Labour would fight the next election as an independent party, although it gave no date for the ending of the Coalition which would continue until victory in Europe. Labour Party leaders lacked confidence in their ability to win a mandate from the people in the post-war world, believing that Churchill's popularity would secure victory for the Tories. Yet the cracks between the parties were widening. Then there were quarrels over the future of the electricity industry, and over iron and steel, and now the disputes were no longer private. In April 1945 Bevin and Bracken criticised each other openly and, despite last minute appeals by Churchill to keep the Coalition going, Labour withdrew and an election was called for July.

5.9   Cartoon by David Low, *Evening Standard*, 12 April 1945

JUST A BIG HAPPY FAMILY

In the cartoon, the book which Beaverbrook is holding is entitled, *Unarmed Combat.* Round the table from left: Attlee, Morrison, Bevin, Churchill, Bracken, Beaverbrook, Anderson, Amery.

Questions

1   With reference to **5.8(a)** and **(b)**
   (i) what do you understand by the phrases 'by a side wind' [**5.8(a)**, **lines 22, 24**], 'on the Bench' [**5.8(b), line 2**]?
   (ii) why, according to Dalton, do both parties distrust the rationing scheme?

2   How do **5.8(a)** and **(b)** illustrate
   (i) the divisions between the political parties?
   (ii) the manner in which wartime pressures and circumstances affected the way government decisions were made?

3   What evidence do these extracts [**5.8(a)** and **(b)**] give of the type of influence which swayed the Cabinet and Churchill in particular?

4   Churchill was sometimes accused of being a dictator in his dealings with his Cabinet. Is there any evidence of that here?

5   Does the fact that these extracts [**5.8(a)** and **(b)**] are from a Labour Minister's diary affect the way a historian might use them in attempting to ascertain how Churchill's government worked? Justify your answers.

6   Look at cartoon **5.9**.
   (i) Comment on the way the representatives of the political parties are seated around the table.
   (ii) Compare Attlee's and Churchill's appearances. What do you think Low is attempting to suggest by this?

7   Could a historian use a cartoon such as this as evidence of what was happening in government? Consider, with reference to cartoons known to you, the way they can both mislead and inform historians.

8   Discuss the extent to which party rivalries were a factor in the wartime government of Britain.

Yet, for all the tensions in the Coalition, it is the general consensus which is significant. Churchill was able to concentrate on winning the war and not on managing his government. He was not a dictator although he had his court favourites, for example Bracken, Lindemann and Beaverbrook. Churchill's reputation has survived the assessments of most post-war historians and, although his faults are readily acknowledged, there appears to be general acceptance that only he could have done the job for which he felt destiny had prepared him.

Churchill as military strategist

Churchill himself placed greatest importance on his role as a military strategist. As Minister of Defence (a post he created), he presided over meetings of the three Chiefs of Staff and was personally involved in all major and minor military decisions [5.10]. Service Ministers became administrators rather than policy-makers,[7] and the War Cabinet rubber-stamped Defence Committee decisions.

Churchill's role as military strategist raises some interesting questions. How effective and competent was he? Did he bully his commanders into precipitate and disastrous action? In retrospect were his strategic decisions the right ones or did they have a Gallipoli tinge to them?[8] Some contemporaries took a sceptical view of his abilities [5.6]. One of the many policies which has been severely criticised by later historians was his support for strategic bombing of Germany. Basil Liddell Hart commented that this 'was like throwing pebbles against an opponent strong enough to throw boulders in reply. As a strategic policy it amounted to nothing more than slow suicide.'[9] Yet one could counter this with the view that Britain had no other way of retaliating against Germany in 1940 and Churchill was not alone in believing that German morale could be broken in this way.

More serious, perhaps, are the criticisms made of the manner in which he harassed his Generals, for example Wavell, encouraging him into making a disastrous attack on Tobruk on 15 June 1941 [5.11]; and the way in which he seriously misjudged the Japanese threat, refusing to allow Pound to abandon Egypt to defend Singapore. However, Ismay, Churchill's representative and spokesman when the COS Committee met without him, stated in his memoirs that he did not once overrule his military advisers on a purely military question. It is now acknowledged that, ironically, on some decisions Churchill was too deferential towards his Generals, and in some campaigns (e.g. Greece 1941) he was less optimistic and precipitate than his advisers. Moreover, his overall grasp of global strategy, his ability to see long-term possibilities, his wide ranging interest in new types of warfare and certain military decisions he took (e.g. his persuasion of Roosevelt and the American Generals to postpone D Day to 1944 and to carry out 'Torch' in North Africa instead), are admired even by his critics.[10]

Here are some examples of the types of evidence historians use in
assessing Churchill as a military leader:

5.10   Diary of John Colville (Private Secretary to Churchill), 29 May 1940

Winston's ceaseless industry is impressive. He is always having
ideas which he puts down on paper in the form of questions and
despatches to Ismay or the CIGS for examination. Sometimes they
relate to matters of major importance, such as the measures to be
taken against invasion, or the provision of more aeroplanes, and   5
sometimes they relate to quite trivial questions. This is the sort of
thing: 'General Ismay. Inquire into the number of German guns now
trophies in this country and whether any can be reconditioned for
blocking exits from beaches against tanks conceivably landed
thereon.' Another today asked whether wax could be supplied to   10
troops to put in their ears in order to deaden the noise of warfare.

John Colville, *The Fringes of Power, Downing Street Diaries*, 1985

5.11   Note from General Wavell to CIGS (Chief of Imperial General Staff), 28 May 1941

All available armoured strength, which will be the deciding factor,
is being put into 'Battleaxe'. Various difficulties are delaying reconsti-
tution 7th Armoured Division. Earliest date for beginning of forward
move from Matruh will be 7 June and may be later.

I think it is right to inform you that the measure of success which   5
will attend this operation is in my opinion doubtful. I hope that it
will succeed in driving enemy west of Tobruk and re-establishing
land communications with Tobruk. If possible we will exploit success
further. But recent operations have disclosed some disquieting features. Our armoured cars are too lightly armoured to resist the fire of   10
enemy fighter aircraft, and, having no gun, are powerless against the
German eight-wheeled armoured cars, which have guns and are
faster. This makes reconnaissance difficult. Our Infantry tanks are
really too slow for a battle in desert, and have been suffering considerable casualties from the fire of the powerful enemy anti-tank   15
guns. Our cruisers have little advantage in power or speed over
German medium tanks. Technical breakdowns are still too numerous.

We shall not be able to accept battle with perfect confidence in spite of numerical inferiority, as we could against Italians. Above factors may limit our success. They also make it imperative that adequate   20
flow of armoured reinforcements and reserves should be maintained.

Quoted in **Winston Churchill**, *The Second World War*, Vol 3, *The Grand Alliance*, 1950

5.12(a)   Telegram from Churchill to Wavell

I venture once again to emphasize that the objective is not the reaching of particular positions, but the destruction by fighting of the armed force of the enemy wherever it may be found. As your force diminishes, so should his. He has a far longer line of communications than you and must be in greater difficulties about supply, especially   5
of ammunition.

PM's personal Telegram, T 278, War Office no. 71086, 9 June 1941, PREM 3/287/1. Quoted in Martin Gilbert, *Finest Hour*, 1983

5.12(b)   Wavell replied:

His communications are little more difficult than mine

Telegram 0/71957, 10 June 1941, quoted in Martin Gilbert, *Finest Hour*, 1983

Questions

1   From your own knowledge of the military situation, why was Churchill so eager to secure a victory in the desert in June 1941?
2   What would you deduce was the purpose of Wavell's note [5.11]?
3   What argument did Churchill use [5.12(a)] to overcome Wavell's objections to making an attack?
4   The attack on Tobruk in June 1941 was a disaster. Does the limited evidence here allow you to attribute blame? Can you find any independent evidence to support your conclusion?
5   How do 5.10 and 5.11 illustrate Churchill's role as a military strategist?
6   Is there any evidence in these extracts that Churchill refused to heed advice and was he wise to do so?

Churchill saw himself as a Warlord but had he been no more than that he would not have become a myth and a legend in his lifetime. His obsessive aim, victory at all costs, enabled him to rise above petty inter-party squabbles; he was simply not interested in party differences when he had the great task of defeating Hitler. For the most part, his colleagues took their political tone from him. In a final estimate, what was his role in wartime? At a time of great military disaster in 1940 and during later setbacks and apparently insurmountable difficulties, he never abandoned his conviction that Britain would win. It was an illogical conviction but one which history proved right. To a certain extent that must be the final touchstone in any attempt to assess his role in the Second World War.

References

1 P. Addison, *The Road to 1945*, Jonathan Cape, 1975
2 P. Adelman, *British Politics in the 1930s and 1940s*, CUP, 1987
3 D. Irving, *Churchill's War*, Veritas, 1988
4 A. Briggs, *The History of Broadcasting in the United Kingdom*, Vol. 3, The War of Words, OUP, 1970, p.4
5 A. J. P. Taylor, *The Warlords*, Hamish Hamilton, 1977
6 R. Lewin, *Churchill as Warlord*, Stein and Day, New York, 1973, p. 133
7 R. Blake, *The Decline of Power*, Granada, 1985, Paladin edn, p. 239
8 This refers to an unsuccessful attack on the Dardanelles in 1915 for which Churchill was blamed
9 B. Liddell Hart, in A. J. P. Taylor *et al.*, *Churchill: Four Faces and the Man*, Allen Lane, 1969, p.188
10 e.g. B. Liddell Hart, in A. J. P. Taylor *et al.*, *Churchill: Four Faces and the Man*, Allen Lane, 1969, p.192

6 The economy and the Second World War

The short-term effect of war upon the British economy was to transform it, not least in the way the government assumed control over all aspects of labour, production, prices, wages and consumption, following the pattern set down in the previous conflict. Several textbooks provide comprehensive general accounts of these trends[1] and the first part of this chapter provides examples of the types of statistics used by historians attempting to interpret the economy. The questions which follow are partly factual and are designed to give the reader some idea of the types of information which can be extracted from this kind of evidence. Further questions then encourage direct observation and comparison. The second part of the chapter looks at ways in which the wartime economy was viewed by contemporaries and later historians, specifically their attempts to interpret the long-term effects of the wartime experience upon Britain's economic performance after 1945. Readers will find a definition of a wartime economy in extract 2.1 (p.30).

In terms of measurable cost, the Second World War was more expensive than the First. Expenditure in the First has been estimated at £11,325 million, in the Second at £28,000 million.[2] The demands of total war forced the government to abandon pre-war economic constraints and to adopt a policy of directing all aspects of Britain's economy towards victory regardless of the long-term consequences. For most civilians the wartime economy meant sacrifices; rationing, higher taxation, loss of freedom in job choices and, in many cases, conscription not just into the Services but into essential war work. The state exercised more control over its citizens' lives than ever before. All these effects of war can be measured with statistics, the tool of the economic historian [6.1–6.7]. For example, there were gains (greater levels of employment [6.2] and increased earnings [6.3]), and there were losses (reduced exports [6.6] and increased borrowing and mounting debts [6.7]).

Yet it is too simplistic to regard the effects of the war as something which can be measured in terms of a balance sheet with losses stacked against gains. Some of the long-term effects are, by their very nature, incalculable; for example, the extent to which under-investment in transport and housing affected key areas of the economy in the post-war world. Nor are all these 'hidden' effects necessarily negative ones. There is a trend amongst some historians to stress the economic benefits to Britain of increased technology and improved production techniques [**6.9**]. Even the conversion of British industry to munitions can be seen as having beneficial effects [**6.8**]. Moreover, public perception of war and its effect on the economy was by no means a totally negative one [**6.10, 6.11**]. Yet it could be argued that one of the most important effects of the war on Britain was in the legacy of complacency it left which encouraged the public and the post-war government to believe that Britain, having mobilised so effectively for war, could afford to devote its new-found efficiency towards developing a welfare state. The public was encouraged to believe British wartime production had been good, but was this in fact the case? Corelli Barnett [**6.12**] has argued that British production merely confirmed traditional bad practices and this legacy, combined with a belief that the public deserved a welfare state after all their sacrifices, condemned British economic performance after the war to a disastrous downward spiral of under-investment in productive capacity and over-consumption in terms of state benefits.

An added complication for any student studying this topic is the need to take into account, not only the effect war had on other countries' economies, but also the extent to which it strengthened or reduced longer-term trends going back, in some cases, to the beginning of the century or even before. Such factors are beyond the scope of this book but should not, however, be overlooked in any final assessment of the topic.

Statistics alone can be used to paint a depressing picture of Britain's wartime economy:

6.1

The impact of the Second World War on the British economy was
more profound than that of the First World War. Between 1939 and
1945 Britain sustained an accumulated deficit on current account of
some £10,000 million. In order to finance this (not to mention an
extra £100 million in foreign and gold reserves), she had received   5
£5,400 million in lendlease and mutual aid from the USA and
Canada, sold £1,000 million of her most lucrative pre-war foreign
investments, requisitioned £100 million of private gold and dollar
balances and increased the volume of short-term overseas liabilities
(mainly in sterling) by a massive £3,700 million. On the domestic   10
side, there had to be added the costs of internal disinvestment
amounting to £3,100 million. Altogether, according to Kirby[3]
'approximate calculations carried out by the Treasury indicated that
by the end of 1945 one-quarter of the country's pre-war wealth had
been liquidated as a direct consequence of Britain's commitment to   15
the Allied war effort.'

Alan Sked, *Britain's Decline*, 1987

Questions

1   (i) What was 'lendlease' [**6.1, line 6**] and when had it started? Why
        was it regarded as necessary?
      (ii) What were 'short-term overseas liabilities' [**line 9**]?
2   Using **6.1**, draw up a list of the ways mentioned here of how Britain
      financed the war.
3   What conclusions is the reader being invited to make about the long-
      term effect of these statistics upon post-war Britain?

Employment and the standard of living

6.2

Distribution of labour force of working age in Britain (in thousands)

	June 1939	*June 1941*	*June 1942*	*June 1943*	*June 1944*	*June 1945*
Armed Forces:						
Total	**480**	**3,383**	**4,091**	**4,762**	**4,967**	**5,090**
Men	480	3,278	3,784	4,300	4,500	4,653
Women	—	105	307	462	467	437
Civil Defence, N.F.S. and Police:						
Total	**80**	**383**	**384**	**323**	**282**	**127**
Men	80	324	304	253	225	112
Women	—	59	80	70	57	15
Group I Industries[1]:						
Total	**3,106**	**4,240**	**4,990**	**5,233**	**5,011**	**4,346**
Men	2,600	3,140	3,285	3,305	3,180	2,891
Women	506	1,100	1,705	1,928	1,831	1,455
Group II Industries[2]:						
Total	**4,683**	**4,845**	**4,983**	**5,027**	**5,100**	**5,191**
Men	4,096	3,856	3,763	3,686	3,710	3,762
Women	587	989	1,220	1,341	1,390	1,429
Group III Industries[3]:						
Total	**10,131**	**8,283**	**7,520**	**6,861**	**6,574**	**6,752**
Men	6,387	4,524	3,943	3,430	3,232	3,368
Women	3,744	3,759	3,577	3,431	3,342	3,384
Registered Insured Unemployed:						
Total	**1,270**	**198**	**87**	**60**	**54**	**103**
Men	1,013	100	61	44	40	68
Women	257	98	26	16	14	35
Ex-Service men and women not yet in employment:						
Total	—	—	—	**20**	**20**	**40**
Men	—	—	—	13	14	27
Women	—	—	—	7	6	13
Working population:						
Total	**19,750**	**21,332**	**22,056**	**22,286**	**22,008**	**21,649**
Men	14,656	15,222	15,141	15,032	14,901	14,881
Women	5,094	6,110	6,915	7,254	7,107	6,768

Note: The figures include men aged 14–64 and women aged 14–59, excluding those in private domestic service. Part-time women workers are included, two being counted as one unit.

[1] Group I covers metal manufacture, engineering, motors, aircraft and other vehicles, shipbuilding and ship-repairing, metal goods manufacture, chemicals, explosives, oils, etc.

[2] Group II covers agriculture, mining, national and local government services, gas, water and electricity supply, transport and shipping.

[3] Group III covers food, drink and tobacco, textiles, clothing and other manufacturers, building and civil engineering, distribution trades, commerce, banking and other services.

Ministry of Labour and National Service and Central Statistical Office, adapted from W. K. Hancock and M. M. Gowing, *The British War Economy*, HMSO, 1949

6.3

Prices and wages

Year ending	Weekly wage rates: estimated increase in all industries[1] (1 Sept 1939 = 100)	Average weekly earnings in certain industries[2] Oct 1938 = 100	Cost of living 1 Sept 1939 = 100	Price index of total consumers' expenditure 1938 = 100	Import prices 1938 = 100	Export prices 1938 = 100	Wholesale prices Aug 1939 = 100
Sept 1939	100	—	100	—	—	—	108
Dec 1941	123–124	146	130	134	164	152	159
Dec 1942	132	165	129	143	179	178	164
Dec 1943	137–138	179	128	147	188	191	166
Dec 1944	145–146	176	130	150	195	197	170
June 1945	148–149	180	132	—	NA	NA	173
Dec 1945	152–153	174	131	153	195	194	173

NA = Not available

[1] Some small industries are omitted.
[2] The figures represent the average earnings before deduction of income tax or insurance. Administrative and clerical workers and other salaried persons are excluded.

Central Statistical Office, adapted from W. K. Hancock and M. M. Gowing, *The British War Economy*, HMSO, 1949

6.4

Personal expenditure on consumers' goods and services at 1938 prices (in £ million)

	1938	1941	1942	1943	1944	1945
Food	1,287	1,036	1,086	1,061	1,120	1,136
Alcoholic beverages	285	287	267	270	274	297
Tobacco	177	196	206	204	205	225
Rent, rates and water charges	491	502	497	498	503	506
Fuel and light	197	205	199	187	193	198
Household goods	288	163	123	107	100	122
Clothing	446	275	273	247	275	279
Books, newspapers & magazines	64	61	63	67	73	77
Private motoring	127	30	17	8	8	25
Travel	163	148	174	186	188	215
Communication services	29	27	31	37	42	40
Entertainments	64	75	87	89	90	94
Other services	483	418	374	350	343	369
Other goods	177	131	109	110	113	120
Income in kind of the armed forces	17	98	106	136	152	146
Total of above items	4,295	3,652	3,612	3,557	3,679	3,849
Adjustment	−7	19	28	34	27	72
Total	4,288	3,671	3,640	3,591	3,706	3,921

Cmd. 7371 and Central Statistical Office, adapted from W. K. Hancock and M. M. Gowing, *The British War Economy*, HMSO, 1949

6.5

Proportion of personal income required to meet taxation (in £ million)

	1938	1941	1942	1943	1944	1945
Personal income	4,884	6,508	7,200	7,721	8,072	8,411
Direct tax payments	439	770	879	1,145	1,328	1,394
Indirect taxes on consumption	611	1,045	1,199	1,282	1,294	1,359
Less subsidies to consumption	− 36	− 137	− 168	− 188	− 202	− 249
Total tax payments out of personal income	1,014	1,678	1,910	2,239	2,420	2,504
Tax payments as a percentage of personal income (%)	21	26	27	29	30	30

Note: The rise in the proportion of tax payments to private income was not all due to increases in rates of taxation; it also reflected the increased consumption of highly taxed goods and services – beer, tobacco, entertainments.

Cmd. 7371 and Central Statistical Office, adapted from W. K. Hancock and M. M. Gowing, *The British War Economy*, HMSO, 1949

Questions

1   Look at table **6.2**.
    (i) What type of industry declined as a result of war?
    (ii) What types of industry recruited most workers during the period 1939–45?
    (iii) What total percentage of the working population was engaged in non-productive work in 1939 and 1945?
    (iv) What total percentage of the labour force was unemployed in 1939 compared with 1945?

2   With regard to **6.2**,
    (i) what are the uses to which a historian could put this table in attempts to gauge the effect of the war on the British economy?
    (ii) what are the limitations of using such a table?

3   What evidence is there in **6.4** that war affected public consumption?

4   How could a historian use **6.4** to deduce the effect war had on British production?

5   Using all the evidence given in **6.2–6.5**, consider what evidence there is for a rising or falling standard of living in wartime Britain. What other types of evidence could you use?

6   'The most important force making for an improvement in the working class position in the Second World War, was the increase and greater progressiveness of taxation.'[4] In what way do the statistics support this statement?

The national economy

6.6

Exports of produce and manufacture of the
United Kingdom

Year	Value as recorded (in £ million)		Index of volume 1935 = 100	
	Including munitions	Excluding munitions	Including munitions	Excluding munitions
1938	470.8		98	
1941	365.4		55	
1942	391.4	271.3	52	36
1943	337.5	233.5	42	29
1944	328.3	266.3	38	31
1945	434.5	399.3	49	45

Note: As the figures up to the end of 1941 do not show munitions separately, it is impossible to get comparable figures.

Board of Trade, adapted from W. K. Hancock and M. M. Gowing,
***The British War Economy*, HMSO, 1949**

6.7

Central Government expenditure, revenue and borrowing
(in £ million)

Calendar years	Expenditure	Revenue	Borrowing	Revenue as percentage of expenditure
1938	1,040	893	147	86
1941	5,052	2,172	2,880	43
1942	5,457	2,635	2,822	48
1943	6,047	3,139	2,908	52
1944	6,078	3,328	2,750	55
1945	5,583	3,293	2,290	59

Cmd. 7371 and Central Statistical Office, adapted from W. K. Han-
cock and M. M. Gowing, *The British War Economy*, HMSO, 1949

Questions

1   Why might the figures in **6.6** and **6.7** together alarm government economists in 1945?

2   What were the sources of revenue the government could call upon in wartime [**6.7**]? How might some of them have been diminished and others increased by wartime economic changes?

3   From your further reading as well as the evidence contained in this chapter:
    (i) Why are exports important to Britain's twentieth century economy?
    (ii) Lendlease ended on 17 August 1945. Explain how it affected the British economy [see also **6.1**].

4   Consider the proposition that statistics alone give a one-sided and simplified view of any historical issue.

You might like to compare these statistics with those in Chapter 2 (p. 36) on the First World War.

Contemporary and post-war perspectives

Certainly the wartime experience cost Britain dear in terms of lost markets and increased debts, but was this all? Corelli Barnett[5] has argued that the war reinforced traditional British weaknesses in the economy, such as overmanning and too many small production units. At the same time, he says, it created an attitude of complacency about economic achievements on the home front and a desire for welfare reforms which channelled British post-war energy and material wealth into a disastrously non-productive welfare state, at the expense of industrial productive capacity.

However, it is doubtful whether war can be blamed for all Britain's post-1945 economic troubles. Other factors such as mismanagement of the economy by pre- and post-war governments, lack of investment in industry, and weaknesses in Britain's competitive performance abroad since the beginning of the century are a few of the many reasons cited for Britain's relatively poor economic performance from 1945 to 1980.

Some historians even argue that the war had beneficial effects on the economy [**6.8**].

6.8   Postan, writing an official history of the war, set a trend in optimistic assessments:

> In everyday discussions the making of munitions is regarded as a
> dissipation of national resources. Yet not everything was a setback
> and a waste.
>
> In the first place, a large volume of new industrial capital was
> created. In the national accountancy of the war years, government   5
> expenditure on buildings, plant and machinery for the munitions
> industry was lumped together with other items of government expen-
> diture, as if it was as fully 'consumed' during the year as the other
> war-stores. There was thus nothing in the accounts to set off against
> the running-down of the capital assets of civilian industry, and the   10
> figure for 'disinvestment', i.e. the net losses in the productive capital
> of the country, was put very high. Yet investment in the munitions
> industry was bound to add to the country's capital resources. Most of
> the industrial buildings erected in wartime have since been occupied
> by post-war industries; a very large proportion of the machinery not   15
> worn-out physically at the end of the war (and assuming a ten-year
> life for machine tools most of the general tools installed during the
> later years of the war still had several years of life before them) found
> post-war employment. Public utilities are, of course, outside the
> scope of this study, but it should be noted here that some of them,   20
> and especially the electrical supply industry, had to grow to match
> the needs of the growing munitions industry.
>
> In the balance, more important still have been certain other less
> tangible gains.

The numbers of insured persons in certain industries, June 1939 and November 1946

Industry	No. insured in June 1939 (in thousands)	No. insured in November 1946 (in thousands)	Percentage increase (%)
Non-ferrous metals manufacture	55.9	87.8	57.1
Shipbuilding and ship-repairing	144.7	219.8	51.9
Constructional engineering	49.0	66.5	35.7
Electric cables, apparatus, etc.	195.9	265.5	35.5
Explosives, chemicals, etc.	174.3	235.5	35.1
Scientific instruments	48.3	65.0	34.6
Marine engineering	52.2	70.2	34.5
General engineering	704.7	944.3	34.0

The increase in the labour force of certain industries was accompa- 25
nied by the spread of new skills among the working population. The
number of workers in the engineering industry in general, and more
especially the number in such key occupations as those of draughts-
men and tool-room operatives, was in 1946 much larger than that of
1939. The supply may still be inadequate in 1952, but the shortage is 30
merely a sign of the continued expansion of the metal-working trades.
In some of the heavier and dirtier branches of engineering, such as
foundries, critical shortages of labour may have developed. But these
were only to be expected in years of 'full employment', and have
moreover led a number of firms to mechanise and clean up the work 35
in their foundries to the lasting advantage of themselves and of
industry in general.

Indeed the changes in methods and processes of industry and in
attitudes of managers, though least tangible of all the developments,
have perhaps been the most remarkable. The momentum of the rising 40
efficiency of management which underlay the soaring output of munitions in the later years of the war was bound to continue into the
years of peace. The historian of post-war industry will not fail to
notice the evidence of new managerial attitudes and techniques. He
may or may not be inclined to contrast them with the managerial 45
sloth of the early twentieth century, but he will have to relate them
and ascribe them to the experiences of the war years.

M. M. Postan, *British War Production*, HMSO, 1952

Sidney Pollard blames Britain's relative decline on her poor investment
record arising from a decision to maintain the value of sterling. He too
saw the wartime experience in a positive light:

6.9

At the end of the war, when Britain had emerged as one of the
victorious great powers helping to shape the peace, she was still
among the richest nations of the world, ahead by far of the war-
shattered economies of Europe. On the continent, only the neutrals,
Sweden and Switzerland, were better off than Britain, and elsewhere 5
only the United States and Canada. Britain was among the technical
leaders, especially in the promising high technology industries of the
future: aircraft, electronics, vehicles. The problem that exercised the
statesmen of the day was whether the rest of Europe, even its

industrialised parts, would ever be able to come within reach of, let   10
alone catch up with, Britain.

Nor was that lead a temporary fluke, a result of the more destructive effects of war on the continent. On the contrary, the British lead in 1950 was fully in line with that of 1938: and even more so with that of earlier decades, when the British position had been firmly in   15
the van of Europe. It had a solid and traditional foundation.

Sidney Pollard, *The Wasting of the British Economy,* **1984**

Such assessments echo the view often presented by the wartime media:

6.10

TANKS Record Smashed by Twenty Per Cent

By RONALD CAMP

In the Ministry of Supply yesterday a staff of statistics' experts, analysing the results of "Tanks for Russia" week, stared at each other.

They could not believe their own figures.

The statisticians checked and cross-checked each other's figures.

Yes they were true. The seemingly impossible had happened.

IN SEVEN TREMENDOUS DAYS BRITISH TANK WORKERS HAVE ADDED 20 PER CENT. TO THE ALL-TIME TOP RECORD SET UP THE WEEK BEFORE.

Not only the tank workers ended a week of triumph. The aircraft Industry finished the best week in the best production month of the war.

They had turned out more planes, from small trainers to great bombers, than ever before.

The spares Industry, vastly important if planes are to be in constant and unfailing use, also topped its record production week.

Guns too: Said the manager of the factory, "There is only one way to tell how the workers – 80 per cent. women – have been going to it this past week –they went Hell for Leather."

News Chronicle, **29 September 1941**

6.11

You have probably come to believe – through hearing it often
repeated – that it will take a long time to pay for this war, and that
we shall be a very poor nation, long after it is finished. If you stop to
think for a moment you will realise how distorted this is. Just think
what makes up the wealth of a country. It is the country's natural   5
resources, its factories, its labour or skill. Realising that this is so, ask
yourself why we should be faced with poverty. To be sure, we are
forced to use our natural resources now by turning them into guns,
and all kinds of means of destruction. But we are having to pay for
this wasteful kind of production at this very moment by the sacrifices   10
we have to make – increased taxation, rationing etc. Indeed, there is
good reason to think that we ought to be paying a more drastic price
at the moment for our essential immediate duty of winning the war.
Once the war is over, once we have completed our immediate task,
there is most certainly the danger that many of our factories may   15
have been destroyed. But we are building new ones, and it will be
mainly a matter of turning them over from the production of destructive weapons to the manufacture of goods for use. Moreover, the
amount of skill available to us ought to have increased enormously as
the result of the war. Before we have gone much further, it will be   20
essential to train millions of workers now unemployed, or engaged on
non-essential industries, in the production of war materials. All these
will be added to the ranks of those who can turn out in peace time
the kind of goods which will be of use or enjoyment to mankind.
Therefore, our ability to produce need not have been greatly dimi-   25
nished, and could have even increased. If our foreign assets will have
decreased, again there will be in our hands the means to replenish
them.

**Extract from an article 'Work For All', by a tutor at Balliol College,
Oxford, in *Picture Post*, 4 January 1941**

Questions

1   From **6.8**, identify
    (i) the weaknesses Postan exposes in using statistics.
    (ii) the 'less tangible gains' from war [**lines 23–24**].

2   Do you agree with Postan that there was 'managerial sloth' [**6.8, lines 45–46**] in the early twentieth century and that the war saw improvement in management techniques? Give reasons for your answer.

3   On what grounds does Postan argue that investment in the munitions industry was beneficial to Britain's economy after the war?

4   How much of Postan's argument [**6.8**] is based on unproven assumptions and does this invalidate it?

5   From reading **6.10** and **6.11**:
   (i) what impression would contemporaries have been given of British wartime production?
   (ii) why were these types of articles published in the media?

6   How might a historian of the British war economy use **6.10** and **6.11**?

7   With reference to **6.8, 6.9** and your wider reading, examine the advances made by Britain in technology during the war years.

Some of the assumptions made in the previous extracts have been challenged. Was production so efficient? Did management practices really change for the better? Were the British encouraged by their wartime successes to be too complacent? Take the example of the aircraft industry, often held up as an example of British success in war upon which she could build after 1945. Corelli Barnett, a modern historian writing in the 1980s, has made the point that:

6.12

> Because the Spitfire certainly equalled the Messerschmitt BF 109 in overall performance as a fighter aircraft, it does not follow that Vickers-Supermarine could have sold it successfully overseas in commercial competition. On the contrary, since the Spitfire took two thirds more man hours to build than the Messerschmitt, it would have been priced out of the market ...   5

Of the radio industry, one of the new technological industries in which Britain is supposed to have excelled in the war, Corelli Barnett comments that it suffered from

> ... a galloping attack of the classic British industrial disease – fragmentation of resources and effort, overlaps in production design, batch production virtually by hand, utter want of standardisation of parts and components.

Corelli Barnett, *The Audit of War*, 1986

Question

1   To what extent and in what ways have Barnett's comments under-
lined weaknesses in the arguments put forward in documents **6.8** and
6.9?

To a certain extent, as these documents have attempted to suggest, the
view historians take depends very much from which angle they
approached the topic. Any student of this theme should therefore
approach the topic with an open and critical mind aware that
unquantifiable factors such as the way the general public perceived
the economy and the effect this had on the post-war world may have
been as important in the long run as measurable statistics such as
production figures.

References

1   For example, J. Stevenson, *British Society 1914–45*, Penguin, 1984,
pp.444–51; H. Pelling, *Britain and the Second World War*, Fontana, 1970
2   J. Stevenson, *British Society 1914–45*, Pelican, 1984
3   M. W. Kirby, *The Decline of Britain's Economic Power since 1880*, Allen and
Unwin, 1981
4   A. Milward, *The Economic Effects of the Two World Wars on Britain*, Macmillan, 1984, p.42
5   C. Barnett, *The Audit of War*, Macmillan, 1986

7 Society in the Second World War

The Second World War transformed lives; there were few who could escape at least some wartime changes; rationing, mobilisation of civilian workers, conscription, evacuation, the Blitz, blackout regulations, increased employment opportunities. Such changes have been comprehensively examined in several excellent books such as Angus Calder's *The People's War*.[1] The long-term consequences of war are, however, less obvious and more controversial. Henry Pelling[2] argues that on the whole the experiences of 1939 to 1945 merely served to confirm the traditional features of society such as the Press, Parliament, the political parties, the civil service, local government and the law. Others such as Marwick and Addison see the experiences of 1939 to 1945 as decisive in bringing about change in some areas, though confirming traditional mores and institutions in others:

> Those who accept the imperfections of human systems, and who appreciate that change is not necessarily always in one direction, will perhaps recognise that even without the drama and tragedy of an occupation and resistance, nonetheless the Second World War did have a considerable impact on the British people.[3]

Other historians such as Stevenson emphasise the role the war played in accelerating previous social, political and economic trends:

> Once again, however, the experience of war served as much to intensify existing social developments as to stimulate new ones. Most of the features emphasized by war, such as greater state control of the economy, increased intervention to provide social welfare, the development of a more collectivist and egalitarian style of government, the stimulus to science and the arts, and the opening of British society to wider cultural influences, notably from the United States, had already been foreshadowed in the years before 1939. In a sense, the war marked a deceptive discontinuity in the social history of Britain.[4]

In attempts to come to terms with the problems in understanding this effect of war, some historians resort to models, for example Marwick's four tier one[3] (see also the introduction to this book, pp. 1–3). Others such as Addison[5] concentrate upon one element, here the Labour victory in 1945, and try to trace its origins to the social and psychological effect of war.

Students seeking to understand the effect of war upon society are thus faced not only with several theories but a confusing array of approaches to the subject. It is proposed, therefore, to concentrate on three areas in which war had an impact on society: evacuation; the development of the Welfare State; and the role of women. Students should bear in mind that these are but three examples of the way war affected society, and other developments such as education (the Butler Education Act of 1944), and town and country planning (a new Ministry in February 1943), should not be forgotten. Nor should the impact war had on cultural topics such as art, literature, music, drama and philosophy be neglected in any general survey of war's effects. For the most part, though, while the world about them was so uncertain, the British public took refuge in the familiar rather than the new, and the period 1939–45 witnessed little change in the arts.

Evacuation

The choice of evacuation as a topic to illustrate the impact of war upon society is not an arbitrary one. Certain experiences such as rationing and the blackout affected the population more uniformly but their impact was restricted to the war or the immediate post-war years. Other wartime experiences such as the Blitz and conscription may have altered individual lives for ever, but are rarely seen as having long-term effects upon society as a whole. Evacuation, which failed in its long-term purpose and involved only a minority of Britain's inhabitants is, nevertheless, held up as an example of a short-lived wartime experience which helped to alter society's perception of itself and therefore its post-war structure. The media publicity given to the transport of some illiterate, unhealthy and unmannerly children to the homes of middle-class rural England has been seen as more of a catalyst than other wartime social experience in bringing about a resolution to improve inner-city life. There was a new determination to demolish slums, provide free health and welfare services and improve educational opportunities for the working classes.

Evidence for all these claims is, however, difficult to find. Certainly evacuation made public some of the worst abuses of the slum areas but it is impossible to gauge exactly what its effect was in relation to other factors which helped to bring about social change. (See also the next section of this chapter, the Welfare State, page 106).

Evacuation was not compulsory. Nevertheless, with bombing raids expected as soon as war broke out, it was popular at first. Between 1 and 4 September 1939 nearly 1½ million school children were evacuated from urban areas and, by the end of another week, 2 million more had joined them. Throughout the period 1939–42 about 4 million children spent anything from a few days to several years as evacuees. Yet these statistics are misleading. Although 80 per cent of London parents had signed for their children to be evacuated, more than half London's children stayed at home, even in September 1939. Many returned to the cities by Christmas 1939 because there were no bombing raids and, at the height of the London Blitz, it has been estimated that between 200,000 and 300,000 children were in the target areas.[6] Pregnant women and mothers with young children, another group evacuated in the first weeks of the war, also drifted back to the urban areas in large numbers. Overseas evacuation, begun in earnest after Dunkirk and discouraged by Churchill, never amounted to more than 20,000. It ended in September 1940 with the sinking of the *City of Benares* and the loss of 84 lives. Thus, although evacuation no doubt saved many children,many more endured the rigours and traumas of bombing raids.

There were, no doubt, some who would have preferred the trauma of the Blitz to the experience of evacuation, although at first the media suggested evacuees were going to a rural idyll. Consider the following.

7.1

BILLETING
"Compulsory Powers Now in Force"

WE have received the following official communication from the Mayor of Cambridge (Ald. A. A. Spalding):–

The public must realise that compulsory powers of billeting have been given to the local authority and are now in force.

Put quite simply it amounts to this: Enough voluntary offers have been received to take in all the children who are coming in school parties. Provided the householders keep their undertakings, there should be no difficulty with this class of refugee. Payment for children (unaccompanied by an adult) who are received in houses will be at the rate of 10s. 6d. per week where one child is taken and 8s. 6d per week for each child where more than one child is taken. This payment is for full board and lodging and will be made by the Government.

The second class, due to arrive on the second and third days are mothers with young children and expectant mothers. Householders will be required to house these women and children. The payment is 5s. per week for each adult and 3s. per week for each child. This payment is for lodging only (with the use of the water supply and sanitary conveniences, and, it is hoped, cooking arrangements). The adult refugee will be responsible for her own and children's food.

Third class, the voluntary helpers from the evacuation areas, will be housed. They will be working full time in the Borough. The payment for them is 21s. per week for each person to cover board and lodging and will be paid by the Government.

Cambridge Daily News, 1 September 1939 – *now the Cambridge Evening News*

7.2   Evacuees arrive at Cambridge: scene at the station

Cambridge Daily News, 1 **September 1939** –now the *Cambridge Evening News*

7.3   25,000 LONDONERS HAPPY ON THE HILLS

Between 25,000 and 30,000 Government paying guests sat down to
dinner with their hosts yesterday in the villages and towns . . . of the
Chiltern Hills in Buckinghamshire.

. . . There was a helping hand for everybody. No mother was allowed   5
to carry any bundle, however small, except her baby.

Smiling patient

One little boy who has lived for four years in a London hospital
arrived smiling happily in a steel jacket.

Tenderly he was lifted into a big car by his host and a chauffeur,   10
given a drink of milk and a batch of comics, and propped up with
cushions before being driven away with his mother and baby brother. . .

At every home, whether cottage or big house, where cars stopped
to discharge the strangers and their luggage, women were waiting
with open arms and a smile of welcome.   15

The poorer the guests the warmer was their reception. At several
houses children were fitted out with clothes from the wardrobe of the
hostesses' own children.

The owner of a big house in a park 800 feet up has given it over to the Londoners and moved with his wife and one servant to the lodge . . . 20

In a one-street village Alf, from Brick Court, Aldgate, put this anxious query to his big sister as they started off to explore the woods and the meadows:–

"Are you sure you know the name of this street in case we get lost?" . . . 25

News Chronicle, 4 September 1939

7.4 From the Notebook of a Billeting Officer

I'm sorry, we can't take a child; my husband keeps his fishing tackle in the spare room.

No, the maids would give notice at once.

I'm afraid not. You see my wife's expecting a happy event quite soon.

I know it looks as if we have room, but mother has only just left, and my aunts are due any day now.

Only if she's a Theosophist.

No. My husband disapproves of the whole idea of evacuation.

I can't manage if she's any fancy religion.

We are reserved for officers.

I'll only take her if she's got no parents.

Yes, if she is a hard worker, a neat seamstress, a good cook and quick on her feet.

Well, we're sleeping five in the kitchen now, but if you can find a corner to fit them in, you're welcome . . .

The doctor says my nerves couldn't possibly stand it . . .

Frankly I can't be bothered.

Sorry, sir, but what with my husband's snoring, it just wouldn't be fair on the kid. 5

Certainly not. My house is nicely furnished.

My husband has got a much better scheme. He keeps writing to the papers about it. 10

I'll take her, but it must be clearly understood that the dogs come first.

Not a London child. The things we've heard about London children . . . 15

I'm sorry, but I just can't do with the War at all.

Who is it, dear? The Billeting Officer. Well, say mother's out . . . 20

Certainly. I can't help feeling it might be my little Doris in need of a home.

Lilliput, 1939, reproduced in Kaye Webb (ed.), *Lilliput goes to War*, 1985

7.5   Memories of evacuation

Along with her mum, dad and sister of 19, Joan Tyson (now
Lowe), who was 21 at the time, found herself sharing her home with
two boys aged six and nine. It was a far cry from the poor area of
Manchester they had left behind:

Each night was spent in de-lousing these two little boys, as they   5
were infested with lice. With newspapers spread out on the table, a
small toothcomb and a good light, it was a case of who could collect
the most lice between my sister and me. They did not appear to
know the use for a knife and fork as they never sat down to a meal at
the table and lived on sandwiches. When [they were] out playing,   10
their mother lowered their food down on a rope as they lived in a
flat. It seemed to us one long battle to get them to stay put at the
table when eating a meal, as they seemed to prefer eating under the
table and would disappear at the slightest chance. When their parents
came from Manchester to see them, arriving by train after lunch,   15
their first call was the public house, so they were always merry when
they reached us late in the afternoon.

Their father would always sing for us, standing before the fire-
place. He was usually in good voice and this 'entertainment' would go
on for some time. My mother found this embarrassing but my sister   20
and I would be stifling our laughter till we ached with the effort.

Ben Wicks, *No Time to Wave Goodbye,* **1988**

Questions

1   Compare the two newspaper articles [7.1 and 7.3] on evacuation.
  (i) On what factual details, if any, do they agree?
  (ii) How does their tone differ?
  (iii) For what purpose(s) could a historian deduce they were written?
  (iv) Is one more useful than the other to a historian attempting to
      find out what happened during evacuation?

2   Photograph 7.2 is typical of those published in almost all newspapers
  at the time. Does it provide evidence of:
  (i) the type of child evacuated?
  (ii) the way evacuation was carried out?
  (iii) the effect evacuation had on the individuals concerned and/or
     society?
  (iv) anything else?
     Explain your answers.

3   Why should a historian treat photographs published in newspapers
     and magazines as a different type of evidence from those taken by
     private individuals?
4   Consider the tone of document **7.4**.
     (i) Do you think the reader is meant to take it seriously?
     (ii) Does it reveal anything about English society in 1939?
5   Compare the impressions given in **7.1–7.3** of the public's response to
     evacuation with those given in **7.4**. In what ways are they similar and
     dissimilar?
6   What evidence is there in **7.5** of social deprivation? Does this docu-
     ment help to explain attitudes in **7.4**? Give reasons for your answer.
7   Are all five extracts [**7.1–7.5**] of equal value as evidence about evacua-
     tion? Justify your answer.
8   'The evacuations helped to publicize the big city squalor; and so it
     can be said that they contributed greatly to the social changes of the
     post-war period.'[6] Do you consider that any of the sources here
     support this statement? Would it be possible to find evidence to
     prove or disprove the assumption made here that social change was a
     direct result of evacuation?

The Welfare State

One of the interesting questions raised by the experiences of 1939–45 is
the extent to which they created Britain's Welfare State. It is usually
argued that war accelerated a trend, already established as far back as
the pre-1914 Liberal governments, of growing state responsibility for its
citizens; a responsibility it was increasingly called upon to fulfil in the
1930s. In this context war is seen as hastening change in three main
ways. Firstly, it provided a climate of opinion which *expected* welfare
reforms at once, instead of just *hoping* for them in some prosperous, but
remote, future. [Contrast **7.6** with **7.7** and **7.8**.] Secondly, as Britain's
survival in part depended upon the ability of her citizens to endure
deprivation, war created a belief amongst governed and governors alike
that the more equitable sharing of resources was desirable. Thirdly, state
control over the wartime economy for the purpose of winning the war
demonstrated that the machinery for such a redistribution of wealth was
available to any post-war government prepared to retain and develop it.
The consensus between governed and governors enabled certain measures to be taken in wartime (for example, the abolition of the Means Test
in 1941) and provided the post-war Labour government with a mandate
to bring about radical reforms.
     For the purposes of this book we have adopted a broad working
definition of what is meant by a Welfare State, accepting Bruce's

explanation that it is 'the sum of efforts of many years to remedy the practical social difficulties and evils of a modern system of economic organisation . . .'[7]

More specifically the Welfare State is concerned with 'formal schemes to compensate for loss of earnings through sickness, unemployment and old age, and a health service to provide medical care for all regardless of means' and it 'implies . . . a degree of collectivism, with the state forming national policies in the interest of the community as a whole . . .'[8]

Historians who accept such wide definitions trace the origins of this type of state back to the Liberal reforms before the First World War, or even earlier. Certainly welfare provision 1939–45, ideas in the Beveridge report, and the measures undertaken by the post-war Labour government were not new. Winston Churchill, when Liberal President of the Board of Trade, had advocated a 'national minimum', and the inter-war years had seen the introduction of several measures such as the extension of the 1911 Insurance Scheme in 1920 and 1921, which owed less to wartime experiences ('Homes Fit for Heroes'), than to a steady growth in popular and intellectual demand for social reform intensified during periods of social and economic distress.

The 'Next Five Years' group, established in 1934, was one of several similar organisations in which interested members met to draw up proposals for intellectual solutions to poverty. They were by no means all left-wing politicians. The signatories of 'The Next Five Years' [7.6] included such diverse individuals as Eleanor Rathbone (Independent MP), Professor Julian Huxley, Siegfried Sassoon, H. G. Wells, Dame Sybil Thorndike, Sir Arthur Pugh (ex-Chairman of the TUC) and Harold Macmillan (later Conservative Prime Minister 1957–63).

Below is an extract from their plan which is typical of the types of material produced in such quantities in the 1930s:

7.6

Within the present century the development of the Social Services, designed to set a lower limit below which poverty and destitution shall not go, has been rapid and extensive. There is a system of unemployment insurance, of unemployment assistance for those who have exhausted their right to insurance, and a system of provision for   5
the elderly or invalid poor; there is a National Health Insurance scheme and a variety of other health services; there are free old age pensions at 70, besides pensions for the widows and orphans of insured workers; there is an education system which provides for every child up to the age of 14 and for many beyond; and there are   10
subsidies in aid of working class housing . . . the total expenditure on

the Social Services has risen in 25 years from £63 millions to £443
millions. The total cost of these services in 1931–2 to the national
finances and to local rates was over £260 millions, and the National
Health Insurance scheme ... embraces nearly 19 million people.   15
    Nevertheless, we believe that there is room both for improvement
and for advance ... there are several extensions of the scheme which
are badly needed. One of these – the provision of allowances for the
dependants of sick or disabled workers – would not cost more than
about £2½ millions, ... Another extension – the provision of medical   20
benefits for the dependants of the insured workers ... should clearly
be high on the list of advances to be made over the next few years ...
The scope of the National Health Insurance might well be extended
to the 'black-coated' workers above the present exemption limit ...
    Each (Social Service) ... reacts on the others. Educational progress   25
is of great social value in itself; old age pensions relieve the misery of
unsupported old age; but both have a further effect in helping to
diminish the pressure on the labour market. Anything which im-
proves the nutrition of the poor will diminish the calls on health
insurance. Every Social Service has an influence on others ...   30
    Our Social Services have been separately enacted and they are
separately administered, often by different departments of state. The
proposal has sometimes been made that they should be amalgamated
into a single scheme under a single administration. Whether this
somewhat ambitious proposal is practicable or not, we think there is a   35
strong case for much more co-ordination both of finance and of
administration, between the different Social Services than exists at
present.

Next Five Years Group, *The Next Five Years,* **1935**

Questions

1   What, according to 7.6, was the purpose of the Social Services, and
    what improvements were seen to be needed?
2   What were the exact provisions of the various Social Services listed in
    7.6? How effective were they deemed to be, by the authors, in
    relieving social distress and poverty?
3   What major factor is implied in 7.6 to be inhibiting the growth of
    these services?
4   Referring closely to 7.6, explain whether the authors believed their
    suggestions were likely to be accepted.

5   Given the purpose of the document, parts of which are quoted in **7.6**, and its authorship, do you think it presents a realistic impression of the state of the Social Services in Britain in 1935? Justify your opinion.

Many of the inter-war advances were secured by Neville Chamberlain who, as Minister of Health in the 1920s and as Chancellor in the 1930s, effected improvements in health insurance, hospitals, local government, Poor Law Reform and pensions. Yet these were all based on the principle of selectivity; i.e. they applied to certain groups in the population. It was the Second World War which saw the adoption of the principle of universalism as applied to social welfare.

Changes in attitude towards social reform are difficult to monitor and measure but there is general agreement amongst historians that the war altered many people's perceptions of what was both desirable and possible, and this was in no small measure due to developments in public opinion allied to state pragmatism. This was a war in which civilians' health and sense of well-being was as important a national asset as a well-equipped fighting force. Hence, for example, mothers and children under 5 were given free or subsidised milk regardless of their economic position. Evacuation and air raids exposed to the public at large the gross deprivations which some civilians in the front line endured every day regardless of wartime shortages and dangers.

Universality became an accepted principle and the idea that all, regardless of wealth or social status, should be able to benefit from welfare schemes. It is this universality which marks a division between attitudes before 1940 and those after. The experience of war, a people united in common sufferings, sacrifices and purpose, created a hope amongst many, and fear amongst a few, that they were fighting for a better, fairer world [**7.7**]. At a time when Labour leaders were pledged to a political truce, a groundswell of opinion for post-war reforms was encouraged by intellectuals and the media. The Beveridge Report (1 December 1942) gave these general aspirations a specific direction.

This Report, which sold 635,000 copies, was not a revolutionary document, despite the fact that it proposed to establish a national minimum, for it supposed that most of the benefits would be paid for by insurance, and it unified existing schemes rather than created new ones. The Report, nevertheless, was widely welcomed as an official statement which appeared to clarify many aspirations formulated by wartime experiences [**7.7**] and which assumed a certain minimum universal provision in health care.

Before Beveridge outlined his proposals for large-scale social legislation in December 1942, indeed as early as mid-1940, many people had begun to think about the post-war world. The table below shows the results of three Mass-Observation[9] surveys.

7.7   Social changes after the war

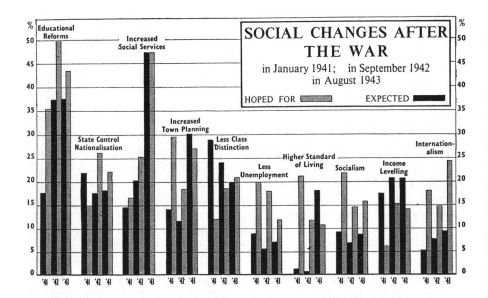

Hope v Expectation

The conflict going on now in people's minds is put into a neat, if over-simplified, nutshell, in the diagram. Three times since 1940 Mass-Observation has asked its National Panel of Observers to out-   5
line their expectations and hopes for social change in Britain after the war. The diagram shows the proportion of this sample who men-tioned various changes:

(a) as expectations

(b) as hopes

in three separate surveys covering three years of war. The figures are   10
strictly comparable since a large proportion of the same individuals answered each time. Though the sample is representative, not of the general population, but of intelligent informed opinion, it shows particularly accurately the ways in which opinion has changed.

Mass-Observation, *The Journey Home*, **Advertising Service Guild, 1944**

Once public interest had been aroused to such a degree by Beveridge, the media, recognising good copy when it saw it, gave it wide coverage. Much of what was published assumed that the Welfare State was well within Britain's economic capacity, and that it was just a matter of planning to carry it out. The following captioned boxes and the picture appeared in an article in a leading popular periodical:

7.8

WHAT WAS PROMISED IN 1918

1. Homes fit for heroes to live in.

2. Health centres; school meals and milk for children.

3. New nursing and maternity services.

4. A higher education programme—continuation schools up to 18.

5. A planned agricultural policy.

6. A proper plan for demobilising the fighting men after the war.

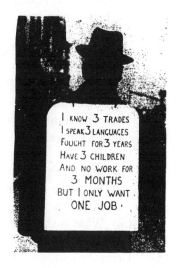

I KNOW 3 TRADES I SPEAK 3 LANGUAGES FOUGHT FOR 3 YEARS HAVE 3 CHILDREN AND NO WORK FOR 3 MONTHS BUT I ONLY WANT ONE JOB

WHY THE PROMISES WERE NOT CARRIED OUT

1. The cost of Government housing schemes was too high because big business insisted on the removal of price controls.

2. Home problems were largely forgotten in the excitement of "making Germany pay."

3. After a temporary boom, "economy at all costs" was put over as a national need.

4. In the scramble for jobs, long-term plans were forgotten.

5. The cry of "no Government interference" carried the day.

6. State factories, shipyards, etc., were returned to "private enterprise."

WHY WE CAN DO BETTER THIS TIME

1. We have a greater industrial machine than ever which can be turned over to peacetime purposes.

2. We have a complete system to regulate and control prices and trade operations.

3. We have the greatest report on the Social Services—Sir William Beveridge's—ever prepared; and full reports on use of land.

4. We have learned that full employment can be maintained by national organisation.

5. The war has helped to break down some class divisions and given us a new sense of community.

6. In our bombed cities, we have the chance to rebuild a better home for ourselves.

Picture Post, 22 May 1943

Questions

1   Study extract **7.7**. In what ways did the sample population's hopes and expectations change in the eighteen months covered by the survey? How do you account for the changes?

2   Look at the way in which this opinion poll was conducted.
   (i) Consider how far the poll would be representative of the population's views as a whole.
   (ii) Given the selective nature of the sample population the poll used, how useful is it to historians?

3   When the Beveridge Report was published in December 1942, 86 per cent of a sample of the general population wanted the report to be accepted and implemented by the government and only 6 per cent wanted it dropped. (Figures given in P. Addison, *The Road to 1945*, p. 217.) Compare this with the percentage given here [7.7] for August 1943 who wanted increased Social Services. How do you account for the differences?

4   Consider **7.8**.
   (i) Summarise the main message of these extracts in a sentence.
   (ii) What are the main anxieties about the future expressed in these extracts?
   (iii) What is the assumption being made here about the way improvements can be carried out?

5   Compare extracts **7.6** and **7.8**. What are the main differences between the two documents and how far do wartime experiences account for them?

6   How many of the promises of 1918 were in fact carried out after July 1945?

7   Consider the view that war did not create the Welfare State but was merely midwife to it.

However, despite its popularity, Churchill did little to promote the Beveridge Report, preferring to concentrate on winning the war. Instead of official government promises the people were fed a diet of exhortatory propaganda from periodicals such as *Picture Post* [7.8]. In 1944, in response to mounting public pressure, the Coalition issued three White Papers which accepted most of the principles of the Report. These White Papers, along with legislation that the Coalition did feel able to pass, the Butler Education Act (1944) and the Family Allowances Act (1945), ensured that by May 1945 the Welfare State was established partly in principle and partly in fact.

Women in war

Assessments of the effect the Second World War has had on women in the twentieth century have become more cautious as the century has progressed. The belief that events of 1939 to 1945 revolutionised women's place in society [7.9] have been replaced by generalisations that war merely accelerated changes already taking place. Some writers have gone so far as to claim that war actually retarded women's emancipation, strengthening their traditional subordinate role and giving them, at best, a temporary passport into a man's world.

This section attempts to give the student some insight into the types of evidence available to historians and the problems of interpreting them. Statistics are often used to support various arguments, and some examples of wages and employment figures are given in 7.10 and 7.12. Public perception of women is difficult to measure in exact terms but Mass-Observation attempted it in 1944 [7.17]. Many pieces of the evidence such as the recruiting poster [7.13] and the cartoon [7.14], are unquantifiable, though, in terms of how far they affected or reflected attitudes to women. Official findings on the type of work women did in wartime [7.10, 7.11] have been included, along with an example of women's own perceptions of themselves as reflected in a magazine [7.16].

As a final point, social change is often brought about by economic factors. Those interested in the former would do well to consult chapter 6, in particular documents [6.2–6.5] which relate to employment, income and expenditure in wartime.

For the American historian, Gordon Wright, the Second World War had an immediate and profound effect on women. Writing in 1968 on the period 1939–45 he commented:

7.9

The rise of women in social status was equally noticeable. The increase in the number of British women employed in industry, government and the armed forces exceeded that of any other warring country. It profoundly altered the role and self image of British women.

5

Gordon Wright, *The Ordeal of Total War,* **1968**

There can be no doubt that as far as numbers of women in employment were concerned there was an increase:

7.10

Number of women in employment 1938–44

Industry or service	Increase (+) or decrease (−) in thousands between 1938 and 1944		Proportions of women included in total of men and women	
	Men (18–65)	Women (18–60)	1938 %	1944 %
Motor vehicle, cycle, aircraft, etc, manufacture and repair	+ 310	+ 330	8	36
Local government service and national fire service (mainly non-permanent staffs)	+ 20 (h)	+ 180 (h)	17 (h)	40 (h)
Chemicals, explosives, paints, oils, etc.	+ 45	+ 170	22	49
Farming and forestry	− 20	+ 90	6	23
Commerce, banking, insurance, etc.	− 140	+ 35	28	62
National government service (non-permanent staffs)	+ 160 (h)	+ 330 (h)	13 (h)	52 (h)

(h) mainly non-permanent staff

Sample of statistics considered by the Royal Commission on Equal Pay, 1945, PRO LAB 17/145

Questions

1   What assumptions are made by Wright [7.9] about the way in which women's status altered 1939–45?

2   Refer to 7.10.
    (i) Suggest reasons why, for each industry or service, men were taken out of some and not others.
    (ii) Which occupations attracted the smallest proportion of women in 1938? Suggest reasons for this.

3   Do you consider that this table [7.10] supports Wright's assumptions? In what ways?

Extract 7.11 is taken from a report by the Employers' Federation. The first paragraph refers to the situation before the war.

7.11

(11) So far as manual workers are concerned, the foregoing factors, (statutory limitations on women's work and the fact that women leave work on marriage) have in practice, brought about, in the great majority of industries, a very clear differentiation of functions between men and women, with the result that, in general, men and   5
women are not employed in the same occupational grades, and, even where the title of the occupation is the same for men and women, the work carried out by the two sexes is not identical.

That position has been partially modified during the war, but, even so, it would appear that in the Engineering Industry, for example,   10
where the largest numbers of women have been taken on during the war, the majority of the new entrants have been assigned to clearly-defined classes of work of a light character which have always been regarded as women's work, and on which some 80,000 women were employed immediately prior to the war.   15

Where the women taken on have been assigned to jobs previously done by men only, the majority are not working under identical conditions with the men, as the jobs have either been broken down, or the women have been afforded greater supervision and assistance.

Report by the Employers' Federation to the Royal Commission on Equal Pay, 1945, PRO LAB 17/145

7.12   The average weekly earnings of men and women, respectively

Date (one week)	Average earnings	
	Men (over 21)	Women (over 18)
	s d	*s d*
Oct. 1938	69 0	32 6
July 1940	89 0	38 11
July 1941	99 5	43 11
July 1942	111 5	54 2
July 1943	121 3	62 2
July 1944	124 4	64 3
Jan. 1945	119 3	63 2
Percentage increase between Oct. 1938 and Jan. 1945	73%	94%

s = shillings
d = pence
12d = 1s (5 new pence)
20s = £1 (100 new pence).

Royal Commission on Equal Pay, paper 285. Statement supplied by the Ministry of Labour and National Service, PRO LAB 17/ 145

Questions

1   According to **7.11**,
    (i) how did women's jobs differ from men's before the war?
    (ii) how was this changed by the experience of war?
2   To what extent, given the nature of the Commission to which it was reporting, would the Employer's Federation be objective in its report?
3   In what ways has this document [**7.11**] modified the impression given in the previous two documents of the way war changed women's status?
4   Referring to **7.12**,
    (i) to what extent did women's earnings improve in relation to men's in the war?
    (ii) suggest reasons why women did not reach parity with men in earnings.

At the beginning of the war little thought had been given by the authorities to the role of women but, by late 1940, it was obvious that they would be needed more and more to replace men on active service. Women, however, were not volunteering quickly enough. In 1941 legislation enabled the government to direct young unmarried women up to the age of 30 towards suitable war work; by the end of the war it covered all women between 18 and 50. Women had a choice between essential war work or a branch of the Services, so the latter had to try to attract 'volunteers' with appeals to their patriotism and sense of duty [**7.13**]. Some people found the notion of women doing essential jobs in the Services difficult to take seriously [**7.14**]; while the women themselves often found it difficult to reconcile domestic chores, which seemed to have grown rather than lessened in wartime, with their patriotism [**7.15**]. Magazines performed a dual role. On the one hand they advocated sacrifice and labour for the good of the state, on the other they urged women not to forget their most important mission, as they saw it, of creating and maintaining a home. When war ended the latter took priority [**7.16**].

7.13

An undated advertisement, printed for HMSO

7.14

" Just there.   15/-, whole head perm."

Cartoon from *Punch* or the *London Charivari*, 10 April 1940

7.15

Save the situation, and the ration coupons, too, with a Mrs. Peek's Pudding! READY MADE for you by the famous house of Peek Frean, from old family recipes. Perfectly sweet, no extra sugar needed.

Mrs Peek's
PUDDINGS

6 *kinds: Xmas, Light Fruit, Dark Fruit, Date, Ginger, Sultana* . . .   1'-

Made by PEEK FREAN & CO. LTD.   MAKERS OF FAMOUS BISCUITS

Advertisement in a woman's magazine, 1942

7.16

These two Wrens are off duty from their real job in the WRNS but in duty time they are learning to be good housewives when they are civilians once more.

Of all civilian refresher courses home-making is the most popular. Wrens visit infant centres and local day nurseries and . . . learn how   5
to handle toddlers or tiny babies.

Wrens who know they are leaving the Service soon can apply to attend a crowded week at a shore-based 'school', where they get down to the job of home-craft in real earnest. They learn cookery, laundry work, simple household repairs. They study interior deco-   10
ration and visit local stores to see what is new in Utility furniture, they learn how to make loose covers and lampshades and rugs and the right and wrong way to paint the home.

Many Wrens have got married or engaged while they've been in uniform, but even those girls who know they will take up civilian jobs   15
are keen to take the home-making course during the last span of their stay in Service.

Woman, 8 December 1945

Questions

1   In **7.13**, are women seen as equal to men? Give reasons for your answer.
2   (i) What do **7.14** and **7.15** reveal about attitudes to women in wartime? How far are these attitudes implied in **7.16**?
     (ii) Does the message they give conflict with that given by **7.13**? In what ways?
     (iii) Discuss whether or not historians should use these types of evidence [**7.13**–**7.16**] when attempting to gauge the effect of war on women in society.

It has been calculated[10] that women did not leave their jobs after the Second World War to the same extent as they did after the First. Milward argues that extrapolation of the trend before 1939 suggests that even as late as the 1950s, a higher percentage of women were in work than would have been had the war not occurred. All this is conjecture. What is significant is the way war did or did not alter attitudes to women and their employment opportunities. Consider the following documents.

7.17(a) Women in men's jobs

Opinion	Percentage holding this opinion		
	Men	Women	Total
Women should be allowed to go on doing men's jobs	30	25	27
Women should not be allowed to go on doing men's jobs	48	43	46
Depends on post-war conditions	19	28	24
No opinion	3	4	3

Mass-Observation, *The Journey Home*, Advertising Service Guild, 1944

7.17(b) Attitude to equal pay for equal work

	Percentage taking this attitude		
	Men	Women	Total
Approve	88	89	89
Disapprove	3	0	1
Miscellaneous	3	0	1
No opinion	6	11	9

Mass-Observation, *The Journey Home*, Advertising Service Guild, 1944

7.17(c)

The lack of strong feeling against women remaining in the jobs which might possibly be needed by men, may perhaps be partly due to the popularity of the woman war worker, which in its turn is partly due to the tremendous amount of government propaganda about the contribution of these women to the war effort. It is not easy for men   5
to take the attitude that 'the women have won the war, but they should be turned out of their jobs as soon as we need them'.

Mass-Observation, *The Journey Home*, Advertising Service Guild, 1944

Questions

1 Compare the percentage of people in **7.17(a)** who held the view that women should not be allowed to do men's jobs after the war with the comment in **7.17(c)**.

2 What does this comment [**7.17(c)**] imply about the way attitudes to women changed as a result of the war? Would you agree that the statistics in **7.17(a)** and **7.17(b)** support this assumption?

There is no doubt that war broke down some barriers to women's advancement in society. Yet, in the end, when the men came home, had attitudes and opportunities really changed that much? In many cases men and women saw the end of the war as a chance to return to their pre-war roles. Because women abandoned their paid employment and went back to unpaid work in the home, the post-war Attlee government had to mount a special campaign to persuade them back into the factories. Most of the advances feminists hail as milestones in women's emancipation came a generation after the war: the Abortion Act (1967), Sex Discrimination Act (1975), Domestic Violence Act (1977); and were as much a result of a new social climate as a memory of wartime experiences. In the end the gains made by women from the war appear, in the context of the whole century, pitifully few.

References

1 A. Calder, *The People's War*, Panther, 1971
2 H. Pelling, *Britain and the Second World War*, Fontana, 1970, p.326
3 A. Marwick, *War and Social Change in the Twentieth Century*, Macmillan, 1974
4 J. Stevenson, *British Society 1914–45*, Penguin, 1984, p. 444
5 P. Addison, *The Road to 1945*, Jonathan Cape, 1975
6 C. Jackson, *Who will take our Children?*, Methuen, 1985
7 J. M. Bruce, *The Coming of the Welfare State*, Batsford, 1961, p.30
8 R. C. Birch, *The Shaping of the Welfare State*, Longman, 1974, p.3
9 Mass-Observation was founded in 1937 by Tom Harrisson and Charles Madge as an independent fact-finding organisation to investigate public opinion and social behaviour in Britain by recording overheard conversations, asking questions and observing behaviour. It relied heavily upon the work of 2,000 amateur volunteers who regularly sent in their diaries for analysis and it also had two units of observers working full time in Fulham in London and Bolton. Despite its claim to be scientific, its results were criticised by some government departments as being subjective and biased. Nevertheless, the Ministry of Information and other official bodies made use of the reports at intervals to try and estimate the state of morale.
10 A. Milward, *The Economic Effects of the Two World Wars on Britain*, Macmillan, 1984, p.36

8 Propaganda and morale in the Second World War

The Ministry of Information

British propaganda in the Second World War laboured under the twin handicaps of government disdain [8.1–8.3] and a misplaced belief in its success in the previous war (see chapter 4). The low status accorded the Ministry of Information, set up in 1939 to deal with domestic propaganda and news censorship, was reflected by the appointment of Lord Macmillan as the first minister, a judge who himself did not understand why he had been given the post. Sir John Reith, replacing him in January 1940, had all his attempts to make the Ministry more than the distribution centre for other departments' publicity and propaganda thwarted by Chamberlain's indifference. Duff Cooper, who replaced Reith in May 1940, as part of Churchill's new Ministry, found himself and his department similarly handicapped. Only when Brendan Bracken, Churchill's friend and adviser, replaced him in July 1941, did the Ministry have an influential leader. As early as July 1940, however, the Ministry had abandoned attempts at exhortatory propaganda, and Bracken continued a pattern already established by which his department concentrated on securing truthful news for the public and issuing information.

The Ministry's low prestige in Whitehall is surprising considering the belief held generally throughout the 1930s in government circles that war would begin with massive air raids on civilians with consequent demoralisation. Few doubted in September 1939 that the determination of each civilian to sustain the trials of war to the bitter end would be a vital factor in securing victory. The government believed, for a short time at least, that good morale was something it could encourage and foster through its propaganda ministry.

Given this belief, and the importance attached to civilian commitment to the war, why did Britain fail to develop a Goebbels, or a propaganda machine similar to that of Mussolini's? Ministry officials believed they had part of the answer. One wrote in June 1941:

8.1

Parliament and Whitehall stand today, in their attitude towards news, publicity, advertising and propaganda, where business stood twenty years ago. Ample lip service is paid to the importance of propaganda in wartime but behind the scenes ... the spirit of scepticism is vocal. Statesmen, civil servants and leaders in the fighting services cannot   5 openly say that news is a nuisance and propaganda a cheap-jack charlatan game but that is what is believed.

Memorandum from A. P. Ryan to the Minister of Information, 4 June 1941, PRO INF 1/857

8.2 The view of Chamberlain and Sir John Reith

The Ministry was an exotic, it pertained to dictatorship.

J. C. W. Reith, *Into The Wind*, 1949

8.3 Duff Cooper comments on Churchill's attitude

When I appealed for support to the PM I seldom got it. He was not interested in the subject. He knew that propaganda was not going to win the war. Looking back, I think he was right, but I could not think so at the time.

Alfred Duff Cooper's autobiography, *Old Men Forget*, 1954

8.4 Disorganisation handicaps propaganda efforts

The over-riding opinion is that the Ministry is still not performing its task with maximum efficiency ... There is presumably some line of policy somewhere in the Ministry. That policy never permeates to the officers charged with dissemination of propaganda. They just get what they can from the general feeling of the country and what they   5 can read in the newspapers. When it comes to distribution they are faced with further difficulties – lack of authority, argument with other divisions, the fight for finance, the proper layout of their material, delays in printing, the fact that so much of the work is handled by amateurs, and so on ...   10

Internal Ministry Memorandum, 1 June 1940, PRO INF 1/533

Questions

1   What do you understand by the phrase 'cheap-jack charlatan game' [8.1, lines 6, 7]?
2   What do you think Reith meant by calling the Ministry 'an exotic' and saying that 'it pertained to dictatorship' [8.2]?
3   What do all these documents [8.1–8.4] reveal about the factors which hindered the issue of effective propaganda in Britain?

The first attempts by the Ministry to issue propaganda were failures. Two red posters were distributed, one of them with the phrase 'FREEDOM IS IN PERIL, DEFEND IT WITH ALL YOUR MIGHT'. The other poster is reproduced below.

8.5   Poster issued by the Ministry of Information, 1939

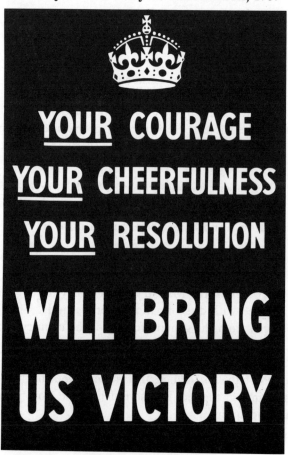

Such posters were considered by Ministry critics to be patronising and too abstract for the general public to understand. Adverse criticism, internal Ministry disorganisation, lack of government guidance, military inaction, all combined to inhibit the production of morale-raising propaganda. The invasion of the Low Countries and the fall of France produced a panic reaction in the Ministry:

8.6

Planning Committee: Papers Circulated
Proposed Plan for Immediate Propaganda

The situation on home morale arising from the French capitulation calls for instant and decisive handling. The immediate essential is to define policy and take action at once on a short-term programme to   5 enable the public to (a) recover without a moment's loss of time from the shock of this news; (b) stand squarely behind the Government in complete determination to fight on to victory.

Peace Offer

Under no circumstances must we allow the rapid and intense   10 rallying of public confidence and patriotism, that must be made to take place in the next few days, to be diverted, delayed or watered down by the red-herring of an illusory prospect of peace, no matter in what guise.

The very word 'peace' must be expunged from the public mind in   15 relation to this transparent snare. It must be given a name where the word peace has no part. 'Hitler's truce trap' is one suggestion . . .

I THE PRESS

General All newspaper proprietors and owners must be immediately approached and told to control the tone of their papers. Sunday's   20 papers were too defeatist and, instead of checking the downward slide of morale, accelerated it. Angles to be plugged with special articles, news stories etc.

(a) They have tried it before and failed – Napoleon, the Armada etc.

(b) The peace offer is a trap   25

(c) For want of anything better we shall have to plug (1) the Navy, (2) the Empire's strength and (3) what a hell of a fine race we must be to have built up both . . .

II   THE BBC

General   There must be some sign of guts in the voices of announcers. This has been suggested for months and yet nothing seems to happen. They can show hate of the Germans and contempt for the Italians in their voices, or if they cannot they must get someone who can. Also the whole programme system needs drastically revising at the moment. Chamber music is no psychological sequel to the fall of Paris. Have we no patriotic tunes or stirring radio speakers? . . .

Entertainments should be coloured. I know the BBC don't like this, but more valuable propaganda can be got across when it appears to be unconscious than directly. In other words dirty cracks against the Germans could be put in musical sketches . . .

A circular should be sent round to leading politicians asking them not to refer to Herr Hitler unless the word 'Herr' is spat out or sneered . . .

Either this is a gentleman's war or it isn't.

Internal Memorandum, 17 June 1940, PRO INF 1/251

Questions

1   Consider the poster [8.5]. It was planned before the war broke out.
   (i) What type of war does the wording suggest was expected then?
   (ii) Do you consider that the two posters issued at this time were appropriate for the British public in the first six months of the war? Give reasons for your answer.
2   Study extract 8.6.
   (i) Referring closely to the document, explain what assumptions were made about the state of morale once the French surrender had been announced.
   (ii) What assumptions are made in the document about the way in which morale could be manipulated?
   (iii) Could you use this document as evidence of the state of public morale in 1940? Explain your answer.
3   (i) Why did Ministry officials feel the BBC had been unsatisfactory in its broadcasts?
   (ii) What evidence is there here as to the extent of Press and BBC freedom?

4   (i) What evidence is there that officials were finding it difficult to think of effective propaganda?

    (ii) What does **8.6** tell the historian about the type of person who worked in the Ministry?

5   None of the suggestions in **8.6** was implemented in June 1940 in Britain but, given the military situation in 1940, do you think the proposed propaganda was appropriate?

Public morale

For a few days in June 1940 it appeared as though Britain might emulate the worst excesses of fascist propaganda. Yet these proposals came to nothing. The government, through the Ministry, did not control either the Press or the BBC. Both types of media were intensely patriotic but were sensitive to consumer reaction. They realised that what the public wanted was a quick and efficient news service and entertainment which enabled them to forget the war. Moreover, it became increasingly obvious to officials that the public was not defeatist. Consider the following report on national reaction to the French defeat:

8.7

> The reaction [to the French armistice] has been one of indignation, which has increased with the announcement of the terms. This is directed more towards the French Government than towards the French people. There is a great deal of vagueness about the future. Except for a small minority, people say that the war must go on. A few say it is better for us to be alone . . .
>
> **Mass-Observation file report no. 224, 23 and 24 June 1940**

The Press, the public and the BBC spontaneously took their tone from Churchill.

8.8

MR. CHURCHILL AND AN INVASION

READY, UNDISMAYED, TO MEET IT

WE SEEK NO TERMS & ASK NO MERCY

LONDON IN RUINS – BETTER THAN ENSLAVEMENT

Mr. Churchill, in a broadcast to British Empire and American listeners last night, reaffirmed his confidence in the determination and ability of this country to resist invasion and, when the time comes, to lift the dark curse of Hitler from our age. He declared:

"Be the ordeal sharp or long, or both, we shall seek no terms, we shall tolerate no parley. We may show mercy, but we shall ask none."

Never before had Britain had an army comparable in quality, equipment or numbers with to-day's. London itself, fought street by street, could easily devour an entire hostile army, and we would rather see London laid in ruins and ashes than that it should be abjectly enslaved.

Looking to the future, Mr. Churchill declared that we must prepare not only for 1941 but for 1942, "when the war will, I trust, take a different form from the defensive in which it has hitherto been bound."

The Prime Minister said that in a week the Royal Air Force and Fighter Command had shot down more than five to one of the German aircraft which tried to attack convoys in the Channel.

Daily Telegraph, 15 July 1940

Questions

1　Summarise public reaction to the fall of France as presented in 8.7.
2　In the light of 8.7 how appropriate do the plans in 8.6 now seem?
3　With reference to 8.8:
　(i) Did Churchill seek to underplay the dangers facing the British people? Explain your answer.
　(ii) Referring closely to the document analyse the ways in which he sought to reassure his listeners.
4　How does this newspaper extract [8.8] help to explain why the government left the Press free to publish news and information as they liked in the war?

Much to the surprise of most officials, morale in general continued to be good. Consider this table produced for inter-departmental circulation in December 1940:

8.9 ESTIMATION OF CONFIDENCE

CONFIDENCE IN	+++	++	+	NEUT	−	−−	−−−
1 Ultimate victory		X					
2 Rightness of our cause		X					
3 A better world							
at home				X			
world wide				X			
4 Our Allies Empire		X					
Allies proper			X				
(America)			X				
5 Form of Government:							
Parliament		X					
Local Government						X	
Regional Administration				X			
6 Leadership:							
PM	X						
Royalty	X						
Ministers			X				
TU Leaders			X				
Local leaders					X		
7 Ourselves:							
Determination	X						
Unity			X				
8 Armed Forces:							
Army		X					
Navy	X						
Air Force	X						
Leadership		X					
Equipment		X					
Strategy			X				
9 Civil Defence:							
ARP	X						
AFS	X						
Medical Services			X				
Restorative Services					X		
12 Integrity of News:							
Radio		X					
Press			X				
Official Communiques					X		
13 Social Justice:							
Law			X				
Wages					X		
Food					X		
Health				X			
Shelters						X	
Evacuation						X	
Position of women				X			
Education						X	

Note The chart above is derived from Home Intelligence reports. In the absence of statistical investigations by random sampling this estimate must be subjective. The categories indicated above could be the subject of further breakdowns: the values given in this chart are convenient generalisations for the week ending Saturday, 7 December 1940.

Home Intelligence Report for Ministry of Information, December 1940, PRO INF 1/251

Questions on 8.9

1   Summarise the findings of this report in a statement of your own about the state of morale in December 1940.
2   Considering the fact that this is a general and subjective view of morale, what other types of evidence would you need to enable you to produce a more comprehensive and detailed view of morale?
3   Which of the factors mentioned here do you think would have caused the government most concern and why?
4   Does the table give any hints that people were concerned with more than just the war? Explain your answer.
5   Why was there so little confidence in local government at this time?
6   Given the government's lack of interest in post-war problems, how far do you think the misapprehensions expressed in no.13 were justified at the time? Three years' later?

It is a modern myth that morale in Britain's blitzed cities was excellent. Consider this contemporary report on Manchester:

8.10

While plenty of Manchester people were determined and courageous, and few were openly defeatist, careful analytical discussions with sample people, confirmed by talks with trained sociologists and social workers ... pointed to a considered private opinion of real depression and despair. Manchester people were definitely on edge, are afraid of   5
the next raid, are beginning really to worry about the future with a feeling of semi-despair. All this is under the surface. It can be overcome by adequate leadership and encouragement. But the present atrophy of the local leadership, consequent upon the wartime system of local government and central authority, is operating here as else-   10
where, to weaken the solidarity of the bigger cities, unless they feel that solidarity naturally ... Manchester is such an unco-ordinated, typographically incoherent, overlapping, jumbled-up nondescript place, that even at the best of times Manchester feeling and a positive Manchester outlook are liable to be lacking ... In the last few   15
months several people have pointed out the tendency for Manchester people to stop work at the slightest siren, sleep all night in shelters long before the Blitz etc ...

The morale of the bombed largely depends on the care they get in
the first thirty-six hours, on how many are steered into rest centres,   20
and how sympathetically they are treated there. The rest centres in
Manchester were almost as unsatisfactory and unprepared, in some
cases, as those in the East End three and a half months before ...
People arrived at the centre about 11pm on Sunday and had their
first cup of tea on Monday morning at 11.30. Bread and jam was   25
handed around between 12 and 1 o'clock. Dinner arrived at about
5pm but many people only had potatoes and gravy. Tea was expected
in the evening but never came ...

**Report by Mass-Observation Group, Home Office files, PRO HO
199/442**

Morale was not easy to assess. Contemporaries disagreed amongst
themselves as to the state of morale in the bombed cities. Consider this,
written by a Home Office official after he had read the previous report:

8.11

Mr Macbane
I have read through the attached reports and they are a most
extraordinary mixture of fact, fiction, and dangerous mischief.
Whoever wrote them has clearly little or no knowledge of the
Civil Defence organisation and has successfully picked up any little
scraps of purely defeatist and mischievous gossip that are going   5
on ...
I presume they are written by what are known as the 'intelli-
gentsia' and I think they would be very much better employed in
doing something useful for the community ...

21 January 1941, Home Office files, PRO HO 199/442

Questions

1   Study extract 8.10.
    (i) How was morale measured?
    (ii) How else could morale have been measured?
    (iii) Why was morale in Manchester considered to have been so
        poor?

(iv) What factors affecting morale were beyond government control? Why was this?

2   Would propaganda, without practical action, have been any help in boosting morale? Justify your answer.

3   Compare this report on morale in the Blitz [8.10] with the way it is presented in other secondary sources you have read.

4   In 8.11, why do you think the official was so sensitive about reports of poor morale?

5   (i) Has your reading of document 8.11 given you any good reason to revise your assessment of document 8.10?

      (ii) Is there any evidence in 8.10 that the criticisms in 8.11 are justified? Explain your answer.

6   Looking back at all the documents in this chapter, draw up a list of reasons why Britain did not develop in the first three years of the war a deliberate propaganda and morale raising policy similar to those pursued by Italy and Germany.

By the end of 1942 the need for a propaganda ministry in Britain had disappeared. Military victories and the publication of the Beveridge report provided the public with the confidence that they could win the war and the vision of a better world for which to fight.

Given the inadequacies of the Ministry's first propaganda attempts and its early abandonment of them, the Ministry's role in securing the truthful dissemination of news appears, in retrospect, to have been its most important function. Until El Alamein (at the end of 1942) the British public had been fed a diet of defeats. Truthful reporting of these was a vital factor in building trust and confidence in Churchill's leadership, and Mass-Observation reports indicated that news was an important factor in building morale.

British newspapers took pride in their freedom and, in a war against fascism and totalitarianism, only in a few dark days of May and June 1940 [8.6] did the Ministry waver in its resolve to allow the Press to report defeats and make criticisms of the government. This decision was made easier by the fact that all major national and regional newspapers were intensely patriotic. Only the communist *Daily Worker* and *The Week* were suppressed (January 1941–August 1942) and this was done on Morrison's insistence, against Ministry of Information advice, although there was no evidence to suggest that these publications were causing alarm and despondency amongst anyone except a few Cabinet Ministers.

The BBC was the most important purveyor of news in wartime. Like the Press it retained its independence and, although its newsreaders were not allowed to alter the wording of official communiques, commentaries on news items and all other programmes remained under the ultimate control of the governors, not the Ministry.

Films and newsreels affected public perception of war almost as much as the BBC. Three-quarters of the adult population went to the cinema in wartime and of these one-third went at least once a week. Each film screening showed short propaganda films (usually five minutes in length) and newsreels. All the films made in Britain in wartime were independently produced, but as the government controlled stocks of raw materials and, as the British Board of Film Censors vetted all films before final screening (not just on moral grounds but for suitability in wartime), it is not surprising that they appear so similar in the patriotic messages they promote.

Newsreels, like films, remained in independent hands during the war but the Ministry of Information controlled what was filmed through the issue of red permits. Cameramen were only granted such permits, needed for military subjects, on condition they submitted all their material for censorship. Such censorship went well beyond that required for military security but, in fact, very few cuts needed to be made. Newsreel representatives were only too anxious to present the acceptable, patriotic view of events. Like the newspapers, this was propaganda and censorship by mutual consent.

Although the Ministry was keen to promote freedom of the printed word it regarded images in newspapers and books as far too dangerous to be published uncensored. Photographs appearing for publication had to be submitted to the censor, and magazines and newspapers soon recognised that those showing too high a proportion of bomb damage or too gruesome a scene of civilian or military carnage were unlikely to be passed. On the other hand, many photographs were not submitted for censorship because of lack of time and much censorship was self-inflicted by these publications who recognised that the public often preferred not to see distressing scenes in explicit detail.

In retrospect what stands out most clearly about propaganda and censorship in the Second World War is the ease with which government, people and the media came to an unwritten and unspoken acceptance of what was right to publish and say in wartime. That is not to say that overt propaganda was not sometimes resented or that the media and the government were in accord all of the time but, nevertheless, it may be concluded that in the field of propaganda as in many other areas such as rationing, the public and the government reached a level of accord about what constituted the common good rarely seen in peacetime.

Bibliography

FIRST WORLD WAR

Primary sources

Diaries and letters

So many memoirs and diaries from the period of the war have been published that it is impossible to refer to them all. Some are more entertaining than others. For example, *Lloyd George, A Diary by Frances Stevenson*, ed. A. J. P. Taylor, Century Hutchinson 1971, is full of insights although regrettably she did not write a diary during 1918. Lloyd George's own *War Memoirs*, Odhams 1938, is a more studied work. Asquith's *Memoirs and Reflections*, Cassell 1928, and Charles Hobhouse's reminiscences, *Inside Asquith's Cabinet*, ed. E. David, Murray 1977, are also very interesting. Lord Beaverbrook's *Politicians and the War*, Thornton Butterworth 1928, contains his own version of the events.

Visual sources

For people within reach of, or able to visit London, unpublished sources are also readily available. The Public Record Office at Kew is accessible to students, as is the British Library, Newspaper Section at Colindale. Magazines and newspapers, national and local, general and specialised, are fascinating sources. The Imperial War Museum holds a rich collection of visual material which is referred to many times in this book. Not all the posters and photographs are on public display; they are, however, available on request, as is access to the Oral History Archive. The public film shows tend to be of material later than 1918, but at the time of going to press, the film *Battle of the Somme* is available on video.

Poetry

The war poems are usually studied for their own intrinsic worth, but they do also contain commentary on the war at home, in particular on the complacency of civilians and the contrast between the jingoistic sentiments at home and the realities of the trenches. Of the many anthologies available, *Poetry of the Great War*, ed. D. Hibberd and J. Onions, Macmillan 1986, is particularly recommended for its clear dating and exposition of the different themes of the poems. The student may also gain valuable insights from a study of the lives of the poets and their creative motivations, for example in *Owen the Poet* by D. Hibberd, Macmillan 1986; or *Wilfred Owen: a*

Biography by J. Stallworthy, OUP and Chatto and Windus 1974. The way in which the poets reflected on reality and in their turn affected perceptions of reality is discussed in P. Fussell, *The Great War and Modern Memory*, OUP 1975.

Secondary sources

Biographies

Secondary sources of a more general nature abound. Biographies of the two Prime Ministers are plentiful. Stephen Koss, *Asquith*, Allen Lane 1976, probably sums up the various views most clearly, but Roy Jenkins' biography, *Asquith*, Collins 1964, is well worth reading, as is C. Hazlehurst's view, both in *British Prime Ministers of the Twentieth Century*, Weidenfeld and Nicolson 1977, and in *Politicians at War, July 1914–May 1915*, Jonathan Cape 1971. Lloyd George is similarly well served. Kenneth Morgan's summary in *Prime Ministers of the Twentieth Century* is a useful one, and his longer account, *Lloyd George*, Weidenfeld and Nicolson 1974, is also clear and readable. John Grigg's accounts of various periods of his life, *My Life*, various volumes, Eyre Methuen 1976–80, are detailed and interesting. Further details about the life, death and virtual canonisation of Edith Cavell are probably most readily attained through *Edith Cavell* by R. Ryder, Hamish Hamilton 1975.

Surveys

R. Blake's *The Conservative Party from Peel to Thatcher*, Fontana 1985, has a very sound section on the period of the First World War. Paul Adelman's two Seminar Studies on the *Rise of the Labour Party*, Longman 1985 revised edn, and the *Decline of the Liberal Party*, Longman 1981, contain a fascinating range of sources; we have endeavoured, where possible, to avoid sources which he has made accessible. T. Wilson's *The Downfall of the Liberal Party 1918–35*, Fontana 1968, tells the story of the Liberal decline clearly and convincingly, and R. McKibbin produces a similarly useful account of *The Evolution of the Labour Party 1910–24*, OUP 1974. The formation of the Coalition is discussed by R. J. Scally in his *Origins of the Lloyd George Coalition*, Princeton 1975, and he summarises various articles in periodicals not always available to schools.
The economy is soundly dealt with in A. Milward, *The Economic Effects of Two World Wars*, Macmillan 1984; a more controversial account is available in *The Decline and Fall of British Capitalism* by P. Hutchinson, Archon Connecticut 1966. Since little has been said about demography in this book, it would be well worth reading R. Mitchison, *British Population Change since 1860*, Macmillan 1977, or N. L. Tranter, *British Population 1740–1940*, Longman 1984. The whole question of the extent to which the war changed society is considered in A. Marwick's *The Deluge: British Society in the First World War*, Penguin 1967.
Objection Overruled by David Boulton, MacGibbon and Keye 1967, is a comprehensive and fascinating study of the anti-war movements and

makes extensive use of contemporary material. As far as cinema is concerned, the only serious study is Nicholas Reeves, *Official British Film
Propaganda during World War I*, Croom Helm and Imperial War Museum
1986, to which several references are made in chapter 4.

SECOND WORLD WAR

Primary sources

Of the wealth of published primary sources on the Second World War the
following are recommended:

Diaries and letters

Churchill's own reminiscences: Winston S. Churchill, *The Second World War*,
six volumes, published by Cassell between 1948 and 1954, provide a good
starting point for the politicians' diaries and autobiographies which have
been published. Amongst the most entertaining and revealing autobiographies, are the following: John Colville (private secretary to Chamberlain,
Churchill and Attlee), *The Fringes of Power, Downing Street Diaries 1939–
1955*, Hodder and Stoughton 1985; Ben Pimlott (ed.), *The Second World
War Diary of Hugh Dalton 1940–45*, Jonathan Cape 1986 (as a Labour
Minister in Churchill's Cabinet, Dalton provides a fascinating insight not
only into the workings of that body, but also into the way Labour Ministers
saw the Coalition). For society generally there are many diaries and autobiographies which give a contemporary picture of wartime Britain. One
such, George Beardmore, *Civilians At War, Journals 1938–46*, OUP 1984,
depicts the life of a struggling clerk living in North London. As a contrast,
N. Nicolson (ed.), *Harold Nicolson, Diaries and Letters 1939–45*, Collins
1967, portrays the life of a man who moved in society and who worked for
the Ministry of Information.

Mass-Observation

Most printed primary sources represent educated groups in society and have
an upper-class bias. One of the best sources of popular attitudes and
experiences in wartime is the Mass-Observation Archive, some of whose
findings are illustrated in the documents; it is held at the University of
Sussex, Brighton. Mass-Observation was not scientific in the modern way in
which opinion polls claim to be. In other words it rarely sought to poll a
statistical sample but rather relied on a team of observers to record their
impressions and reminiscences. Nevertheless, it remains a unique and valuable record of wartime Britain and some of its oral history archives are
easily accessible, for example Angus Calder and Dorothy Sheridan (eds.),
Speak For Yourself: A Mass-Observation Anthology, Jonathan Cape 1984.
There is nothing to stop the interested student from conducting his or her
own history investigation with willing neighbours or relatives; though any
such research, unless carried out methodically and with a large enough
sample, would tend to be too specific to allow for generalised conclusions.

Visual sources

There are several primary visual sources available to students of this period. Jane Waller and Michael Vaughan-Rees, *Women in Wartime*, Macdonald 1987, provides a wealth of primary sources from women's magazines. Marion Yass, *This Is Your War*, HMSO 1983, contains examples not just of posters but also of government propaganda and information literature. Joseph Dorracott and Belinda Loftus, *Second World War Posters*, Imperial War Museum 1972, provide useful examples of visual propaganda. Photographs can be excellent sources of evidence. In Arthur Marwick's *The Home Front*, Thames and Hudson 1976, there is an unusually large number of photographs with several examples of those the censor passed or stamped 'not to be published'. Robert Kee, *We'll Meet Again: Photographs of Daily Life in Britain During World War Two*, Dent and Sons 1984, provides a useful photographic archive.

David Low, *Years of Wrath*, Victor Gallancz 1949, reprinted 1986, contains some marvellous examples of political cartoons.

Films and newsreels

Films are often shown on television and the Imperial War Museum has a regular programme of newsreels, Ministry of Information shorts and, occasionally, commercial films of the two wars. For a student who wishes to view these critically the following are recommended: Anthony Aldgate and Jeffrey Richards, *Britain Can Take It: The British Cinema in the Second World War*, Basil Blackwell 1986; Jeffrey Richards and Dorothy Sheridan (eds), *Mass-Observation at the Movies*, Routledge and Kegan Paul 1987; Philip M. Taylor (ed.), *Britain and the Cinema in the Second World War*, Macmillan 1988.

Selections of primary sources

Finally Richard Brown and Christopher Daniels, *Twentieth Century Britain*, Macmillan 1982, and Paul Adelman, *British Politics in the 1930s and 1940s*, CUP 1987, both contain excellent selections of source materials with questions.

Secondary sources

Biographies

The number of books on Churchill grows yearly. Amongst the best are: Martin Gilbert, *Finest Hour 1939–41*, Heinemann 1983, and *The Road To Victory 1941–45*, 1986; Henry Pelling, *Winston Churchill*, Macmillan 1967; A. J. P. Taylor et al, *Churchill: Four Faces and the Man*, Allen Lane 1969; Ronald Lewin, *Churchill as Warlord*, USA 1973. Two books which break new ground are: David Day, *Menzies and Churchill at War*, Angus and Robertson, Australia, 1986, and David Irving, *Churchill's War, volume 1*, Veritas, Australia, 1987. The former casts interesting light upon the extent to which Churchill's support flagged in 1941. The latter is an unconvincing alternative view of Churchill, presenting him as a cowardly warmonger.

There are too many biographies of political leaders to mention all of them. A few will suffice. Kenneth Harris, *Attlee*, Weidenfeld and Nicolson 1982, and Ben Pimlott, *Hugh Dalton*, Jonathan Cape 1985, provide a political antidote to all Churchill books; and John Colville, *The Churchillians*, contains an insider's view of the great man's advisers and friends.

Surveys

For a general political survey Paul Addison, *The Road to 1945*, Jonathan Cape 1975, is still unrivalled. Henry Pelling, *Britain and the Second World War*, Fontana 1970, deals comprehensively with all the main issues. There are several excellent accounts of society during the period. Angus Calder, *The People's War*, Jonathan Cape 1969, and Norman Longmate, *How We Lived Then*, Hutchinson 1971, concentrate entirely on the war. For a wider view, John Stevenson, *British Society 1914–45*, Penguin 1984, places social and economic developments in a wider perspective. Arthur Marwick, *Britain in a Century of Total War*, Bodley Head 1968, and *War and Social Change in the Twentieth Century*, Macmillan 1974, contain interesting chapters on both wars.

Students wishing to trace the development of the Welfare State in the context of the wartime experience would do well to consult one or more of the following: R. C. Birch, *The Shaping of the Welfare State*, Longman 1974; Maurice Bruce, *The Coming of the Welfare State*, Batsford 1968; Derek Fraser, *The Evolution of the British Welfare State*, Macmillan second edn 1984. Most of the general books on society and the economy have sections on women; a useful specialist book is Gail Braybon and Penny Summerfield, *Out of the Cage*, Pandora 1987. Carlton Jackson, *Who Will Take Our Children?*, Methuen 1985, and Ben Wicks, *No Time To Wave Goodbye*, Bloomsbury 1988, contain a useful mixture of primary source material and secondary comments on education.

The economy is well served by historians. Alan S. Milward, *The Economic Effects of the Two World Wars on Britain*, Macmillan 1984, is excellent. Alan Sked, *Britain's Decline*, Basil Blackwell 1987, surveys the main economic trends from 1870 up to the present day. Corelli Barnett, *The Audit of War*, Macmillan 1986, is a stimulating and readable account of the economic legacy of the war.

The following books on aspects of propaganda and morale are useful: Michael Balfour, *Propaganda in War, 1939–45*, Routledge and Kegan Paul 1979. Balfour worked inside the Ministry of Information and in this book he makes a fascinating comparison of the British and German systems. Ian McLaine, in *Ministry of Morale*, Allen and Unwin 1979, explores the work of the British Ministry of Information in depth. Philip Knightley's *The First Casualty*, Andre Deutsch 1975, is a study of the role of the war correspondent over the last 120 years. For morale at home Tom Harrisson, *Living Through the Blitz*, Collins 1975, and Norman Longmate's *Air Raid*, Hutchinson 1971, both attempt to re-evaluate the state of British morale in the Blitz.

This book list does not seek to be comprehensive. All the books cited here have good bibliographies and the student should use them for further reading.

Index